The Trut... ...nt

"Solomon's 50 snappy chapters are as brisk and addictive as YouTube videos, proving he not only knows what consumers want to buy, but also what readers want to read."

"Michael Solomon's book is filled not only with the key truths of how to understand and reach consumers, but also debunks some of the most pervasive myths that exist in the fields of marketing and consumer behavior. Chock-full of up-to-date, engaging examples, this book's easy accessibility belies the depths of information within. It is one of those books that will produce an 'Aha!' moment every time you pick it up."

J. Alison Bryant, Ph.D.
Senior Research Director,
Digital Research Nickelodeon/
MTV Kids & Family Group

"Michael Solomon's *The Truth About What Customers Want* contains great insights into consumer behavior and is a must-have tool for anyone working in a consumer-driven field. His 50 truths take the guess work out of marketing intelligence and give insight into navigating today's technology-driven world."

Tim Dunphy
Senior Marketing Manager,
Consumer Insights, Black & Decker

THE TRUTH ABOUT

WHAT CUSTOMERS WANT

Michael R. Solomon

© 2009 by Pearson Education, Inc.
Publishing as FT Press
Upper Saddle River, New Jersey 07458

FT Press offers excellent discounts on this book when ordered in quantity for bulk purchases or special sales. For more information, please contact U.S. Corporate and Government Sales, 1-800-382-3419, corpsales@pearsontechgroup.com. For sales outside the U.S., please contact International Sales at international@pearsoned.com.

Printed in the United States of America

First Printing: October 2008

ISBN-10: 0-13-714226-9
ISBN-13: 978-0-13-714226-2

Pearson Education LTD.
Pearson Education Australia PTY, Limited.
Pearson Education Singapore, Pte. Ltd.
Pearson Education North Asia, Ltd.
Pearson Education Canada, Ltd.
Pearson Educatión de Mexico, S.A. de C.V.
Pearson Education—Japan
Pearson Education Malaysia, Pte. Ltd.

Library of Congress Cataloging-in-Publication Data

Solomon, Michael R.

   The truth about what customers want / Michael Solomon.

      p. cm.

   ISBN 0-13-714226-9 (pbk. : alk. paper) 1. Consumer behavior. 2. Consumers--Attitudes. I. Title.

   HF5415.32.S63 2009

   658.8'342--dc22

                    2008007869

Vice President, Publisher
Tim Moore

Associate Publisher and Director of Marketing
Amy Neidlinger

Acquisitions Editor
Jennifer Simon

Editorial Assistant
Heather Luciano

Development Editor
Russ Hall

Operations Manager
Gina Kanouse

Digital Marketing Manager
Julie Phifer

Publicity Manager
Laura Czaja

Assistant Marketing Manager
Megan Colvin

Marketing Assistant
Brandon Smith

Cover and Interior Designs
Stuart Jackman,
Dorling Kindersley

Design Manager
Sandra Schroeder

Managing Editor
Kristy Hart

Senior Project Editor
Lori Lyons

Project Editor
Jovana San Nicolas-Shirley

Copy Editor
Karen Gill

Proofreader
San Dee Phillips

Senior Compositor
Gloria Schurick

Manufacturing Buyer
Dan Uhrig

To my favorite consumers:
Gail, Orly, Amanda, Zach, Alex, and Squishy.

Introduction

The truth is, this book is about people like you. It concerns the products and services you buy and use and the ways these fit into your life. First, a bit of jargon: The field of *consumer behavior* is the study of the processes involved when individuals or groups select, purchase, use, or dispose of products, services, ideas, or experiences to satisfy needs and desires. Consumers take many forms, from an eight-year-old child begging her mother for a Webkinz stuffed animal to an executive in a large corporation deciding on a multimillion-dollar computer system. The items we "consume" can include anything from canned peas to a massage, democracy, Reggaeton music, or a celebrity like Lindsay Lohan.

In its early stages of development, researchers called the field *buyer behavior*, reflecting an emphasis on the interaction between consumers and producers at the time of purchase. Most marketers now recognize that consumer behavior is, in fact, an ongoing process; not merely what happens at the moment a consumer hands over money or a credit card and, in turn, receives some good or service. To build bonds with customers, you also need to have them in mind before they ever contemplate buying your product or service and after they've purchased from you. After all, there are lots of good salesmen who can, as the saying goes, sell ice to Eskimos—but probably not more than once.

Why should managers, advertisers, and other marketing professionals bother to learn about consumer behavior? Very simply, understanding consumer behavior is good business. The basic *marketing concept* states that firms exist to satisfy needs. These needs can only be satisfied to the extent that marketers understand the people or organizations who will use the products and services they are trying to sell so that they can meet these needs better than their competitors.

Understanding consumer behavior is good business.

Consumer response is the ultimate test of whether a marketing strategy will succeed. Thus, knowledge about consumers should be incorporated into every facet of a successful marketing plan. Data about consumers helps organizations to define the market and identify threats and opportunities to a brand. And in the wild and wacky world of marketing, nothing is forever. This knowledge also helps to ensure that the product continues to appeal to its core market.

So, how do we figure out what customers want? There must be 50 ways....

TRUTH

1

Your customers want a relationship, not a one-night stand

Sony blew it. Big time. In 1979, a company engineer cobbled together a personal listening device at the request of a senior executive who wanted to listen to opera during transatlantic plane trips, and the Walkman was born. Although the company invented the mobile music experience and sold over 300 million Walkmans in the process, today's teens see portable cassette players as dinosaurs (assuming they've even heard of cassettes!).

Fast forward to a new century. Apple continues to innovate—but, more importantly, Jobs & Co. created a mystique around the iPod that makes it the epitome of coolness. So much for being first to market! It's not just the functionality of this MP3 player that has consumers packing Apple stores; people bond with Apple not because of what it *does* but because of what it *means.* This story is hardly unique: In virtually every product or service category, the brand that forges a relationship with its users is the one that commands their undying loyalty.

So, what about poor Sony? Of course, the firm has succeeded with many other innovative electronics products, so it's hard to shed any tears over its loss of dominance in the mobile music market. And, to its credit, its engineers haven't given up: As the Walkman craze faded, they conducted research to understand how teenagers actually used portable music players in their day-to-day lives. Eventually, they figured out that they needed to relaunch the product with a removable "Memory Stick" instead of a cassette player so that it works with MP3 files. In 2006, Sony integrated its noise-canceling technology into both the player and the headphones. Its ergonomically designed Walkman Bean MP3 player (which vaguely resembles a curled-up fetus) fits easily into your hand. In 2007, Sony extended the Video Walkman brand by launching its first digital, flash-based video Walkman, the NW-A800.

People bond with Apple not because of what it does but because of what it means.

Despite these heroic efforts, the iPod continues to hold about three-fourths of the digital music player market that Sony once owned. Why? Apple understood from the start what Sony is just starting to get: Don't just focus on hardware enhancements. Build in an ongoing connection with customers by providing them with cutting-edge content to put onto their hardware. Apple's iTunes store accounts for about 70 percent of all online music sales.[1] And through creative advertising but also via aggressive world-of-mouth, cultivate a distinct and desirable "brand personality" that makes

Solid marketer-consumer relationships trump technical prowess every time.

users eager to display their affiliation with your brand for all the world to see. That's why the Sony store is pleasant to visit, but the Apple store is *awesome*—and, for some, practically a religious experience. And that's why solid marketer-consumer relationships trump technical prowess every time.

TRUTH

2

Design it,
and they will come

As manufacturing costs go down and the amount of "stuff" that people accumulate goes up, consumers increasingly want to buy things that will provide thrills and chills in addition to simply doing what they're designed to do. A Dilbert comic strip poked fun at this trend when it featured a product designer who declared: "Quality is yesterday's news. Today we focus on the emotional impact of the product." Fun aside, the new focus on emotional experience is consistent with psychological research that finds that people prefer additional experiences to additional possessions as their incomes rise.

In this design-crazed market, form *is* function. Two young entrepreneurs named Adam Lowry and Eric Ryan discovered that basic truth when they quit their day jobs to develop a line of house-cleaning products they called Method. Cleaning products—what a yawn, right?

But, think again. For years, companies such as Procter & Gamble have plodded along, peddling boring boxes of soap powder to generations of housewives who suffered in silence, scrubbing and buffing, yearning for the daily respite of martini time. Lowry and Ryan gambled that they could offer an alternative— cleaners in exotic scents such as cucumber, lavender, and ylang-ylang that come in aesthetically pleasing bottles. The bet paid off. Within two years, the partners were cleaning up, taking in more than $2 million in revenue. Shortly thereafter, they hit it big when Target contracted to sell Method products in its stores.

> In this design-crazed market, form *is* function.

There's a method to Target's madness. Design is no longer the province of upper-crust sophisticates who never got close enough to a cleaning product to be revolted by it. The red-hot store chain has helped to make designers such as Karim Rashid, Michael Graves, Philippe Starck, Todd Oldman, and Isaac Mizrahi household names. Mass-market consumers are thirsting for great design, and they're rewarding those companies that give it to them with their enthusiastic patronage and loyalty. From razor blades such as the Gillette Sensor, computers such as the Apple, and even the lowly trashcan, design *is* substance.

Even crotchety old P&G is starting to get the idea. Although it's a bit like turning a battleship, Procter & Gamble now recognizes the importance of integrating design into every product initiative. In the "good old days" (that is, a couple of years ago), design was basically an afterthought. Marketing meant appealing to customers in terms of efficiency rather than aesthetics.

Design is no longer the province of upper-crust sophisticates who never got close enough to a cleaning product to be revolted by it.

Now, its CEO wants P&G to focus on what he calls "the first moment of truth"—winning consumers in the store with packaging and displays. As a result, P&G now has a vice president (VP) of design, strategy, and innovation who reports directly to the CEO. Her philosophy sums it up: "Competitive advantage comes not just from patents, but also from incorporating design into products, much like Apple, Sony, or Dell."[2]

3

Sensory marketing— smells like profits

Odors can stir emotions or create a calming feeling. They can invoke memories or relieve stress. One study found that consumers who viewed ads for either flowers or chocolate and who also were exposed to flowery or chocolaty odors spent more time processing the product information and were more likely to try different alternatives within each product category.[3]

Many consumers are getting aggressive about controlling the odors in their environments. This olfactory vigilance has spawned a lot of new products since Glade marketed the first air freshener to suburban families in 1956. Today, younger people are at the forefront of scented air as they take advantage of plug-ins, fragrance fans, diffusers, and potpourri. Sensing a growing market, Procter & Gamble introduced Febreze air products in 2004 and appealed to twentysomethings by making air freshener products seem cool. Scentstories is a Febreze dispenser that P&G designed to look like a CD player, complete with "stop" and "play" buttons that radiate scents rather than music.

Some of our responses to scents result from early associations that call up good or bad feelings.

Some of our responses to scents result from early associations that call up good or bad feelings. That explains why businesses are exploring connections among smell, memory, and mood. Researchers for Folgers found that, for many people, the smell of coffee summons up childhood memories of their mothers cooking breakfast, so the aroma reminds them of home. The company turned this insight into a commercial in which a young man in an army uniform arrives home early one morning. He goes to the kitchen, opens a Folgers' package, and the aroma wafts upstairs. His mother opens her eyes, smiles, and exclaims, "He's home!"

We process fragrance cues in the *limbic system*, the most primitive part of the brain and the place where we experience immediate emotions. One study even found that the scent of fresh cinnamon buns induced sexual arousal in a sample of male students![4] In another study, women sniffed T-shirts that men had worn for two days (wonder how much they paid them to do *that*?) and reported which ones they preferred. The women were most attracted to the odor of men who are genetically similar to themselves, though not too similar. The researchers claimed that the findings were evidence that we are "wired" to select compatible mates, but not those so alike as to cause inbreeding problems.[5]

As scientists continue to discover the powerful effects of smell on behavior, marketers are coming up with ingenious ways to exploit these connections. Ad companies spend about $80 million per year on scent marketing; the Scent Marketing Institute estimates that number will reach more than $500 million by 2016. Sensory marketing is taking interesting turns as manufacturers find new ways to put scents into products, including men's suits, lingerie, detergents, and aircraft cabins. Here are a few recent smelly strategies.

> As scientists continue to discover the powerful effects of smell on behavior, marketers are coming up with ingenious ways to exploit these connections.

- One hundred gas stations in California are trying technology that wafts a coffee aroma at the pump in a bid to tempt its pay-and-go customers into the store for a cup of Joe to go.

- Kraft Foods sponsored a special holiday issue of *People* magazine. Five of its ads in the issue allowed readers to rub a spot to experience the smell of a product being advertised, such as Chips Ahoy and Philadelphia Cream Cheese.

- Mars used scent technology to spread the aroma of chocolate around its M&M's World retail outlets, and it put Pedigree dog food-scented stickers in front of supermarkets and pet stores (presumably to attract hard-core pet lovers and their furry friends).

- A company called ScenAndrea that describes itself as a "multisensory communications" vendor is putting 8,000 scent-delivery systems called Smellavision in stores, including Kroger and Wal-Mart.

- In the summer of 2007, Kentucky Fried Chicken (KFC) launched its new $2.99 Deals in several office buildings by strategically placing a plate of chicken, a side item, and a biscuit in mail carts that pass out interoffice mail. A spokesperson notes that "Mailroom staffers were all fed first so that they would have the strength to deal with the employees clamoring for the KFC." Perhaps the next time you get a letter that's still soggy with gravy, you'll know why.[6]

- To promote the drama series *Cane*, which is set in South Florida where a Cuban-American family runs the Lucia Duque rum and sugar business, editions of *Rolling Stone* included Peel 'n Taste flavor strips that deliver the (nonalcoholic) taste of a fictional Lucia Duque Rum mojito cocktail.

These tactics smell profitable, but beware of stinking the place up in your zeal to reach jaded customers: The California Milk Processor Board (the "Got Milk?" people) had to remove cookie-scented advertisements at five San Francisco bus stops after several groups complained about the smell. The idea was to get passersby to think about cookies, which would then, naturally, lead to fantasies of milk to dip them in. Unfortunately, not everyone got the message; the campaign managed to offend anti-fragrance, anti-allergy, and anti-obesity groups simultaneously. Moo.

TRUTH

4

Pardon me, is that a breast in your Coke?

Most marketers lose sleep about creating messages that their customers will notice as they compete with all the other things vying for their limited attention. Ironically, a good number of consumers appear to believe that marketers design many advertising messages, so the consumers perceive them unconsciously, or below the threshold of recognition. Another word for threshold is *limen* (just remember "the secret of Sprite"), and we call stimuli that fall below the limen *subliminal*. *Subliminal perception* occurs when the stimulus is below the level of the consumer's awareness.

Subliminal perception is a topic that has captivated the public for more than 50 years, despite the fact that there is virtually no proof that this process has any effect on consumer behavior. A survey of American consumers found that almost two-thirds believe in the existence of subliminal advertising, and more than one-half are convinced that this technique can get them to buy things they do not really want.[7] Most recently, ABC rejected a Kentucky Fried Chicken (KFC) commercial that invited viewers to slowly replay the ad to find a secret message, citing the network's long-standing policy against subliminal advertising. KFC argued that the ad wasn't subliminal at all, because the company was telling viewers about the message and how to find it. The network wasn't convinced.

Like this KFC ad, most examples of subliminal advertising that people have "discovered" over the years are not subliminal at all—on the contrary, the images are quite apparent. Remember, if you can see it or hear it, it's *not* subliminal; the stimulus is above the level of conscious awareness. Nonetheless, the continuing controversy about subliminal persuasion has been important in shaping the public's

A survey of American consumers found that almost two-thirds believe in the existence of subliminal advertising, and more than one-half are convinced that this technique can get them to buy things they do not really want.

beliefs about advertisers' and marketers' abilities to manipulate consumers against their will.

If you believe all the hype, marketers are staying busy as they dream up new ways to send out subliminal messages on both visual and aural channels. *Embeds* are tiny figures they insert into magazine advertising by using high-speed photography or airbrushing. These hidden figures, usually of a sexual nature, supposedly exert strong but unconscious influences on innocent readers.

Does this appeal to latent lust actually work? Some limited evidence hints at the possibility that embeds can alter the moods of men who are exposed to sexually suggestive images presented subliminally, but the effect (if any) is very subtle—and may even work in the opposite direction by creating negative feelings among viewers. To date, the only real impact of this interest in hidden messages is to sell more copies of "exposés" written by a few authors and to make some consumers look a bit more closely at print ads—perhaps seeing whatever their imaginations lead them to see.

The possible effects of messages hidden on sound recordings also fascinate many consumers. We see one attempt to capitalize on subliminal auditory perception techniques in the growing market for self-help audios. These CDs and tapes, which typically feature the sounds of crashing waves or other natural sounds, supposedly contain subliminal messages to help listeners stop smoking, lose weight, gain confidence, and so on. Despite the rapid growth of this market, there is little evidence that subliminal stimuli transmitted on the auditory channel can bring about desired changes in behavior.

So, is this stuff worth the effort? Some research by clinical psychologists suggests that people can be influenced by subliminal messages under *very specific* conditions, though it is doubtful that these techniques would be of much use in most marketing contexts. Effective messages must be very specifically tailored to individuals rather than the mass messages that advertisers *need* to create to reach a larger audience. Here are other discouraging factors.

■ There are wide individual differences in threshold levels. For a message to avoid conscious detection by consumers who have low thresholds, it would have to be so weak that it would not reach those who have high thresholds.

15

- Advertisers lack control over consumers' distance and position from a screen. In a movie theater, for example, only a small portion of the audience would be in exactly the right seats to be exposed to a subliminal message.

- The viewer must be paying absolute attention to the stimulus. People watching a television program or a movie typically shift their attention periodically and might not even be looking when the stimulus is presented.

- Even if the desired effect is induced, it operates only at a very general level. For example, a message might increase a person's thirst but not necessarily for a specific drink. Because basic drives are affected, marketers could find that after all the bother and expense of creating a subliminal message, demand for competitors' products increases as well!

The bottom line: Keep looking for those embedded breasts all you want, but don't stop searching for those UFOs either.

TRUTH

5

One man's goose...

Two people can see or hear the same event, but their interpretation of it can be as different as night and day, depending on how the message "speaks" to their brains and what they thought they were going to see. A recent study illustrates the power of expectations. Kids ages 3 to 5 who ate McDonald's French fries served in a McDonald's bag overwhelmingly thought they tasted better than those who ate the *same* fries out of a plain white bag. Even carrots tasted better when they came out of a McDonald's bag—more than half the kids preferred them to the same carrots served in a plain package! Ronald would be proud.[8]

The meaning we assign to a stimulus depends on the *schema*, or set of beliefs, to which we assign it. In a process we call priming, certain properties of a stimulus evoke a schema. This, in turn, leads us to compare the stimulus to other similar ones we've encountered in the past.

Identifying and evoking the correct schema is crucial to many marketing decisions, because this determines what criteria consumers will use to evaluate the product, package, or message. Extra Strength Maalox Whip Antacid flopped even though a spray can is a pretty effective way to deliver the product. But, to consumers, aerosol whips mean dessert toppings, not medication.

One factor that determines how we will interpret a stimulus is the relationship we assume it has with other events, sensations, or images in memory. When RJR Nabisco introduced a version of Teddy Grahams (a children's product) for adults, it used understated package colors to reinforce the idea that the new product was for grown-ups. But sales were disappointing. Nabisco changed the box to bright yellow to convey the idea that this was a fun snack, and buyers' more positive associations between a bright primary color and taste prompted adults to start buying the cookies.

Our brains tend to relate incoming sensations to others already in memory, based on some fundamental organizational principles. These principles derive from *Gestalt psychology*, a school of thought that maintains that people interpret meaning from the totality of a set of stimuli rather than from any individual stimulus. The German word *Gestalt* roughly means whole, pattern, or configuration, and we summarize this term as "the whole is greater than the sum of its parts." The Gestalt perspective provides several principles relating to the way our brains organize stimuli.

- The **closure principle** states that people tend to perceive an incomplete picture as complete. That is, we tend to fill in the blanks based on our prior experience. This principle explains why most of us have no trouble reading a neon sign even if several of its letters are burned out. The principle of closure is also at work when we hear only part of a jingle or theme ("You can take Salem out of the country, but..."). Marketing strategies that use the closure principle encourage audience participation, which increases the chance that people will attend to the message.

- The **principle of similarity** tells us that consumers tend to group objects that share similar physical characteristics. Green Giant relied on this principle when the company redesigned the packaging for its line of frozen vegetables. It created a "sea of green" look to unify all its different offerings.

- The **figure-ground principle** states that one part of a stimulus will dominate (the *figure*), and other parts will recede into the background (the *ground*). This concept is easy to understand if you think literally of a photograph with a clear and sharply focused object (the figure) in the center. The figure is dominant, and the eye goes straight to it. The parts of the configuration that a person will perceive as figure or ground can vary depending on the individual consumer as well as other factors. Similarly, marketing messages that use the figure-ground principle can make a stimulus the focal point of the message or merely the context that surrounds the focus.

The stimuli we perceive are often ambiguous. It's up to us to determine the meaning based on our past experiences, expectations, and needs. A classic experiment demonstrated the process of "seeing what you want to see." Princeton and Dartmouth students separately viewed a movie of a particularly rough football game between the two rival schools. Although everyone was exposed to the same stimulus, the degree to which students saw infractions and the blame they assigned for those they did see were quite different depending on which college they attended.[9]

Consumers tend to project their own desires or assumptions onto products and advertisements.

As this experiment demonstrates, consumers tend to project their own desires or assumptions onto products and advertisements. This interpretation process can backfire for marketers. Planters Lifesavers Company found this out when it introduced a vacuum-packed peanuts package called Planters Fresh Roast. The idea was to capitalize on consumers' growing love affair with fresh-roast coffee by emphasizing the freshness of the nuts in the same way. A great idea—until irate supermarket managers began calling to ask who was going to pay to clean the peanut gook out of their stores' coffee-grinding machines.

Another recent experiment demonstrated how our assumptions influence our experiences. In this case, the study altered beer drinkers' taste preferences simply by telling them different stories about a specific brew's ingredients. The researcher offered bar patrons free beer if they would participate in a taste test. (Not surprisingly, very few refused the offer.) Participants tasted two beers each—one a regular draft of Budweiser or Samuel Adams, and the other the same beer with a few drops of balsamic vinegar added. Although most beer *aficionados* would guess that vinegar makes the drink taste bad, in fact, 60 percent of the respondents who did not know which beer contained the vinegar actually preferred the doctored version to the regular one! But when tasters knew in advance which beer had vinegar in it before they took a swig, only one-third preferred that version.[10]

TRUTH

6

Throw 'em a bone,
and they'll no longer roam

Are we smarter than dogs? How about pigeons or rats? Although (recent episodes of reality TV to the contrary) we certainly hope so, the truth is that, under some circumstances, we respond to companies in much the same way that our "less-evolved" friends do. Behavioral learning theories assume that learning takes place as the result of responses to external events—whether these consist of cheese versus electric shocks at the end of a maze or friends' compliments when we show up at a party wearing a new outfit.

According to the *behavioral learning* perspective, the feedback we receive as we go through life shapes our experiences. We respond to brand names, scents, jingles, and other marketing stimuli because of the learned connections we form over time. People also learn that actions they take result in rewards and punishments; this feedback influences the way they will respond in similar situations down the road. Consumers who receive compliments on a product choice will be more likely to buy that brand again, but those who get food poisoning at a new restaurant are not likely to patronize it in the future.

> We respond to brand names, scents, jingles, and other marketing stimuli because of the learned connections we form over time.

The plot thickens. People also react to other, similar stimuli in much the same way they responded to the original stimulus; we call this generalization a *halo effect*. A drugstore's bottle of private brand mouthwash deliberately packaged to resemble Listerine mouthwash may evoke a similar response among consumers, who assume that this "me-too" product shares other characteristics of the original. Indeed, consumers in one study on shampoo brands tended to rate those with similar packages as similar in quality and performance as well.[11] This process may help to explain the tendency for Chinese marketers to knock off familiar vehicle brand names when they can get away with it. When executives at Shanghai Automotive Industry Corp. failed in their bid to buy the celebrated Rover brand name for a line of cars they were introducing, they called them Roewe instead. Honda Motor Co.

successfully sued a Chinese motorcycle maker for using the name Hongda. More recently, though, a Chinese company called Chery is preparing to export a car to the United States. The company claims the resemblance to Chevy is just a coincidence, as its English name derives from the sound of its Chinese name, Qirui, pronounced *che-ray*, which means, "unusually lucky." That argument is a bit harder to make for a wireless e-mail service that another Chinese company calls Redberry.

Behavioral learning principles apply to many consumer phenomena, ranging from creating a distinctive brand image to the perceived linkage between a product and an underlying need. The transfer of meaning explains why made-up brand names, such as Marlboro, Coca-Cola, Reebok, or Exxon (which a computer generated!) can exert such powerful effects on consumers. These associations are crucial to many marketing strategies that rely on the creation and perpetuation of *brand equity*, in which a brand has strong positive associations in a consumer's memory and commands a lot of loyalty as a result.

Advertisements often pair a product with a positive stimulus to create a desirable association. The choice of a great brand name that will elicit these favorable associations is so important that companies often hire naming consultants to devise a winning selection. These experts try to find *semantic associations* that click because they evoke some desirable connection. That strategy brought us names such as Qualcomm ("quality" and "communications"), Verizon (veritas is Latin for "truth," and "horizon" suggests forward-looking), and Intel ("intelligent" and "electronics"). The name Viagra rhymes with the famous waterfall Niagara. People associate water with both sexuality and life, and Niagara Falls is a honeymoon Mecca.

The conditioning process is what's behind branding and packaging decisions that try to capitalize on consumers' positive associations with an existing brand or company name. We can clearly appreciate the value of this kind of linkage by looking at universities with winning sports teams where loyal fans snap up merchandise, from clothing to bathroom accessories, emblazoned with the school's name. Strategies that marketers base on these ingrained associations include

- **Family branding**—Many products capitalize on the reputation of a company name. Companies such as Campbell's, Heinz, and General Electric rely on their positive corporate images to sell different product lines.

- **Product line extensions**—Marketers add related products to an established brand. Dole, which we associate with fruit, introduced refrigerated juices and juice bars, whereas Sun Maid went from raisins to raisin bread.

- **Licensing**—Companies often "rent" well-known names. This strategy is increasing in popularity as marketers try to link their products and services with popular brands or designers. *Prevention* magazine introduced vitamins, and *Runners World* magazine puts its name on jogging suits.

So, condition your customers—and pass those pigeon pellets, please.

TRUTH

7

Stay in their minds— if you can

It's too bad we can't market to elephants. In a poll of more than 13,000 adult humans, more than half were unable to remember any specific ad they had seen, heard, or read in the past 30 days.[12] How many can you remember right now? Clearly, forgetting by consumers is a big headache for marketers.

As the popularity of the board game Trivial Pursuit shows us, people have a vast quantity of information stored in their heads that is not necessarily available on demand. Although most of the information that enters our memory does not go away, it may be difficult or impossible to retrieve unless the appropriate cues are present. What influences the likelihood that customers will remember a commercial message?

Individual cognitive or physiological factors are responsible for some of the differences we see in retrieval ability among people. Some older adults consistently display inferior recall ability for current items, such as prescription drug instructions, although they may recall events that happened to them when they were younger with great clarity. The recent popularity of puzzles like Soduku and centers that offer "mental gymnastics" attests to emerging evidence that we can keep our retrieval abilities sharp by exercising our minds just as we keep our other muscles toned by working out on a regular basis.

Not surprisingly, recall is enhanced when we pay more attention to the message in the first place. Some evidence indicates that we can retrieve information about a *pioneering brand* (the first brand to enter a market) more easily from memory than we can for *follower brands* because the first product's introduction is likely to be distinctive and, for the time being, no competitors divert our attention. In addition, we are more likely to recall descriptive brand names than those that do not provide adequate cues as to what the product is.

> Although most of the information that enters our memory does not go away, it may be difficult or impossible to retrieve unless the appropriate cues are present.

The way a marketer presents her message influences the likelihood we'll be able to recall it later. The *spacing effect* describes the tendency for us to recall printed material more effectively when the advertiser repeats the target item periodically rather than presenting it repeatedly in a short period. The viewing environment of a marketing message also affects recall. For example, commercials we see during baseball games yield the lowest recall scores among sports programs because the activity is stop-and-go rather than continuous. Unlike football or basketball, the pacing of baseball gives many opportunities for attention to wander even during play. Similarly, General Electric found that its commercials fared better in television shows with continuous activity, such as stories or dramas, compared to variety shows or talk shows, which are punctuated by a series of acts. A large-scale analysis of TV commercials found that viewers recall commercials shown first in a series of ads better than those they see last; this may be due to the tendency for our attention to wander as we endure a commercial break.[13]

Some advertisers today are experimenting with *bitcoms* that try to boost viewers' retention of a set of ads inserted within a TV show. (We call this a *commercial pod.*) In a typical bitcom, when the pod starts, a stand-up comedian (perhaps an actor in the show) performs a small set that leads into the actual ads. This is one way that marketers are trying to integrate a show's contents with commercial messages and increase viewers' involvement with advertising.

Finally, it goes without saying that the nature of the ad itself plays a big role in determining whether it's memorable. One recent study on print advertising reported that we are far more likely to remember spectacular magazine ads, including multipage spreads, three-dimensional pop-ups, scented ads, and ads with audio components. For example, a Pepsi Jazz two-page spread with a three-dimensional pop-up of the opened bottle and a small audio chip that played jazz music from the bottle's opening as well as a scratch-and-sniff tab that let readers smell its black cherry vanilla flavor scored an amazing 100 percent in reader recall.[14]

Short of putting on a Broadway production, what can we do to improve memory for our messages? As a general rule, prior familiarity with an item enhances its recall. Indeed, this is one of the basic goals of marketers who try to create and maintain awareness of their products. The more experience a consumer has with a product, the better use she makes of product information. Also, stimuli that stand out in contrast to their environments are more likely to command attention which, in turn, increases the likelihood that we will recall them. Almost any technique that increases the novelty of a stimulus also improves recall. This explains why unusual advertising or distinctive packaging tends to facilitate brand recall. *Mystery ads*, in which the ad doesn't identify the brand until the end, are more effective at building associations in memory between the product category and that brand—especially in the case of relatively unknown brands.

How about the way a message gets delivered? Is it true that a picture is worth 1,000 words? There is some evidence for the superiority of visual memory over verbal memory; the available data indicate that we are more likely to recognize information presented in picture form at a later time. Certainly, visual aspects of an ad are more likely to grab a consumer's attention. In fact, eye-movement studies indicate that about 90 percent of viewers look at the dominant picture in an ad before they bother to view the copy.[15]

Consumers recall ads with visual figures more often and like them better. Understanding what they said is another story.

But here's the fly in the ointment: Although pictorial ads may enhance recall, they do not necessarily improve comprehension. One study found that television news items presented with illustrations (still pictures) as a backdrop resulted in improved recall for details of the news story, even though understanding of the story's content did not improve.[16] Another study confirmed that, typically, consumers recall ads with visual figures more often and like them better.[17] Understanding what they said is another story.

TRUTH

8

These are
the good old days

The McDonald's fast-food chain is riding a nostalgia wave as the nerdy Ronald McDonald and other icons from the 1960s became hot with young hipsters who are scrambling to score T-shirts emblazoned with the clown or other Mickey D's characters such as Mayor McCheese, the Hamburglar, and Grimace. This peak in nostalgia was no accident, however. The company recently launched a word-of-mouth marketing campaign to boost its uncool image among fashion-conscious young people. It hired the same company that revived other nostalgia figures, such as Strawberry Shortcake, and for the first time licensed the use of its old ad slogans and characters on merchandise. McDonald's sold retro T-shirts in trendy boutiques and started to use pop stars such as Justin Timberlake and Destiny's Child in its ads.

Nostalgia describes a bittersweet emotion where we view the past with both sadness and longing. References to "the good old days" are increasingly common, as advertisers call up memories of youth—and hope these feelings will translate to what they're selling today. That's why marketers like Mickey D's often resurrect popular characters and stories from days gone by; they hope that consumers' fond memories will motivate them to revisit the past. We had a 1950s revival in the 1970s, and consumers in the 1980s got a heavy dose of memories from the 1960s. Today, it seems that popular characters need to be gone for only a few years before someone tries to bring them back. That's the case with the Teletubbies, four characters aimed at children ages three and under that a BBC television show introduced in 1997. Ragdoll, the British company that owns the rights to these lovable (yet strangely creepy) creatures, brought them back with features including a trivia quiz, podcasts, and a Web site at taketheteletubbiestest.com.

> References to "the good old days" are increasingly common, as advertisers call up memories of youth—and hope these feelings will translate to what they're selling today.

Why do consumers relish nostalgia appeals? According to one consumer analyst, "We are creating a new culture, and we don't know what's going to happen. So we need some warm fuzzies from our past."[18] In the aftermath of September 11, 2001, consumers seem to crave the comfort of items from the past even more. Marketers such as Ford, GE, S.C. Johnson, and Sears are sponsoring campaigns that celebrate their heritage. Other companies are reviving once-popular products such as Breck shampoo, Sea & Ski sun-care lotion, St. Joseph's aspirin, and the Care Bears; or they're bringing back themes and characters from old shows to sell new products, as when Old Navy transforms "The Brady Bunch" into "The Rugby Bunch" to push its shirts. A *retro brand* is an updated version of a brand from a prior historical period. These products trigger nostalgia, and researchers find that they often inspire consumers to think back to an era where (at least in our memories) life was more stable, simple, or even utopian—they let us "look backward through rose-colored glasses."

In addition to liking ads and products that remind us of our past, those experiences help to determine what we like now. Consumer researchers created a *nostalgia index* that measures the critical ages during which our preferences are likely to form and endure over time. For example, liking for specific songs appears to be related to how old a person was when that song was popular—on average, we are most likely to favor songs that were popular when we were 23.5 years old. Preferences for fashion models peak at age 33, and we tend to like movie stars that were popular when we were 26 or 27 years old. Men, but not women, also show evidence of nostalgic attachment to cars from their youth.[19]

Products and ads can themselves serve as powerful retrieval cues. Indeed, the three types of possessions that consumers most value are furniture, visual art, and photos. These objects are most likely to jog memories of the past. Researchers find that valued possessions can evoke thoughts about prior events on several dimensions, including sensory experiences, friends and loved ones, and breaking away from parents or former partners. Food can do the same thing. A recent study looked at how favorite recipes stimulate memories of the past. When the researchers asked informants to list three of their favorite recipes and to talk about these choices, they found that people tended to link them with memories of past events such as childhood memories, family holidays, milestone events (such as dishes they only make on special holidays, like corned beef and cabbage on St. Patrick's Day), heirlooms (recipes handed down across generations), and the passing of time (for example, only eating blueberry cobbler in the summer).[20]

Yearbooks are a favorite way to preserve our memories ("What was I thinking with that haircut?"), but traditional albums are giving way to more high-tech solutions such as MyYearbook.com. This Web site allows users to create a profile with separate sections for high school, college, graduate school, and professional life. Students who sign up are linked automatically to others at their school. They can select friends from among their classmates and "autograph" each others' yearbook pages. Users also can vote for the biggest flirt, best athlete, and most popular students. The traditional players in this area, such as Jostens (which sells almost $350 million of yearbooks annually), aren't sure if hard copy albums are obsolete, so they are hedging their bets by offering students a supplemental DVD that lets them add their own music, photos, and videos.

Products are particularly important as markers when our sense of the past is threatened.

Products are particularly important as markers when our sense of the past is threatened as, for example, when an event, such as divorce, relocation, or graduation challenges a consumer's current identity. Our possessions often have *mnemonic* qualities that serve as a form of external memory by prompting consumers to retrieve episodic memories. For example, family photography allows consumers to create their own retrieval cues; the 11 billion amateur photos we take annually form a kind of external memory bank for our culture. A stimulus is, at times, able to evoke a weakened response even years after we first perceived it. We call this effect *spontaneous recovery*, and this reestablished connection may explain consumers' powerful emotional reactions to songs or pictures to which they have not been exposed in quite a long time.

TRUTH

9

Why ask why?

About seven percent of the general population is vegetarian, and women and younger people are even more likely to adopt a meatless diet. An additional 10 to 20 percent of consumers are interested in vegetarian options in addition to their normal fare of dead animals. And more and more people are taking the next step and adopting a vegan lifestyle. Although the proportion of consumers who are vegetarian or vegan is quite small compared to those of us who still like to pound down a Quarter Pounder, big companies are taking notice of this growing interest in vegetarian and cruelty-free products. Colgate recently purchased a controlling interest in Tom's of Maine, and Dean Foods (America's largest processor of dairy foods) bought Silk and its parent company White Wave. The beef industry fights back with its high-profile advertising campaign— "Beef: It's What's for Dinner"—and a Web site to promote meat consumption (beefitswhatsfordinner.com). It's obvious that our menu choices have deep-seated consequences.

The forces that drive people to buy and use products are generally straightforward, such as when a person chooses what to have for lunch. As hard-core vegetarians demonstrate, however, even the basic food products we consume relate to wide-ranging beliefs regarding what we think is appropriate or desirable. In some cases, these emotional responses create a deep commitment to the product. Sometimes people are not even fully aware of the forces that drive them toward some products and away from others. Often a person's values—his or her priorities and beliefs about the world—influence these choices.

Sometimes people are not even fully aware of the forces that drive them toward some products and away from others.

Motivation refers to the processes that lead people to behave as they do. To understand motivation is to understand why consumers do what they do. Why do some people choose to bungee jump off a bridge or compete on reality shows, whereas others spend their leisure time playing chess or gardening? Marketing students are taught from day one that the goal of marketing is to satisfy consumers' needs.

However, this insight is useless unless we can discover what those needs are and why they exist.

Psychologists have worked hard to classify human needs. For example, individuals with a high *need for achievement* strongly value personal accomplishment. These consumers are good prospects for products that provide evidence of their achievement. One study of working women found that those who were high in achievement motivation were more likely to choose clothing they considered businesslike and less likely to be interested in apparel that accentuated their femininity.[21] Some other important needs that are relevant to consumer behavior include the following.

- **Need for affiliation (to be in the company of other people)—** The need for affiliation is relevant to products and services for people in groups, such as participating in team sports, frequenting bars, and going to shopping malls, and it serves to alleviate loneliness.

- **Need for power (to control one's environment)—**Many products and services allow consumers to feel that they have mastery over their surroundings. These products range from "hopped-up" muscle cars and loud boom boxes (large portable radios that impose one's musical tastes on others) to luxury resorts that promise to respond to every whim of their pampered guests.

- **Need for uniqueness (to assert one's individual identity)—** Products can satisfy the need for uniqueness by pledging to accentuate a consumer's distinctive qualities. For example, Cachet perfume claims to be "as individual as you are."

The psychologist Abraham Maslow proposed one influential approach to motivation. He originally proposed that we travel up a hierarchy of needs until (if we're lucky) we attain "peak experiences"; marketers later adapted his framework to understand consumer motivations.

The basic lesson of Maslow's hierarchy is that one must first satisfy basic needs before progressing up the ladder. (A starving man is not interested in status symbols, friendship, or self-fulfillment.) That implies that consumers value different product attributes depending on what is currently available to them. For example, consumers in the former Eastern bloc are now bombarded with images of luxury goods, yet may still have trouble obtaining basic necessities.

Marketers' application of this hierarchy has been somewhat simplistic, especially as the same product or activity can satisfy a number of different needs. For example, one study found that gardening could satisfy needs at every level of the hierarchy:[22]

- **Physiological**—"I like to work in the soil."
- **Safety**—"I feel safe in the garden."
- **Social**—"I can share my produce with others."
- **Esteem**—"I can create something of beauty."
- **Self-actualization**—"My garden gives me a sense of peace."

Another problem with taking Maslow's hierarchy too literally is that it is culture-bound; its assumptions may apply only to Western culture. People in other cultures (or, for that matter, even some in Western cultures as well) may question the order of the levels it specifies. A religious person who has taken a vow of celibacy would not necessarily agree that physiological needs must be satisfied before self-fulfillment can occur. Flaws aside, this perspective reminds us that customers have different need priorities in different consumption situations and at different stages in their lives. The best product in the world won't meet a need that doesn't exist.

The best product in the world won't meet a need that doesn't exist.

TRUTH

10

He who dies with the most toys wins

More than 8.2 million women in 50 countries read versions of *Cosmopolitan* in 28 different languages—even though, because of local norms about modesty, some of them have to hide the magazine from their husbands! Adapting the *Cosmo* credo of "Fun, Fearless Female" in all these places gets a bit tricky. Different cultures emphasize varying belief systems that define what it means to be female, feminine, or appealing—and what is considered appropriate to see in print on these matters. Publishers of the Chinese version aren't permitted to mention sex at all, so articles about uplifting cleavage are replaced by uplifting stories about youthful dedication. Ironically, there isn't much down-and-dirty material in the Swedish edition either—but for the opposite reason: The culture is so open about this topic that it doesn't grab readers' attention the way it would in the United States.

We characterize every culture in terms of its members' endorsement of a value system. Every individual may not endorse these values equally and, in some cases, values may even seem to contradict one another. (For example, Americans appear to value both conformity and individuality and seek to find some accommodation between the two.) Nonetheless, it is usually possible to identify a general set of *core values* that uniquely define a culture. Core values such as freedom, youthfulness, achievement, and materialism characterize American culture.

> It is usually possible to identify a general set of *core values* that uniquely define a culture.

Did we mention materialism? This value refers to the importance people attach to worldly possessions. During World War II, members of "cargo cults" in the South Pacific literally worshiped cargo salvaged from crashed aircraft or washed ashore from ships. These people believed that their ancestors piloted the ships and planes passing near their islands, so they tried to attract them to their villages. They went so far as to construct fake planes from straw in hopes of luring the real ones!

We may not worship products to that extent, but many of us certainly work hard to attain our vision of the good life, which abounds in material comforts. Most young people can't imagine a life without cell phones, MP3 players, and other creature comforts. Materialistic values tend to emphasize the well-being of the individual versus the group, which may conflict with family or religious values. That conflict may help to explain why people with highly material values tend to be less happy.

Of course, not all of us are materialists and, indeed, large numbers of consumers are trying to reduce their reliance on possessions by *downshifting*. They are learning to get by with less, avoid the use of credit cards and, in extreme cases, live totally "off the grid" without using commercial services. One of the most famous downshifters is the so-called Ditch Monkey, a dapper young lawyer who created quite a stir in the UK when he spent a year living in a ditch on the outskirts of London (and, of course, blogging about his experience). He explained, "I want to make people think about how much they consume that is not necessary. I am trying to prove it is possible to do everything you normally do, maintaining a full existence, while cutting back. I have realized I can lead my life without television, carpets, sofa, electricity, chairs, tables, a fridge, and a freezer." After getting over her initial surprise at this abrupt lifestyle change, his girlfriend eventually grew proud of the statement he was making. However, she notes (in typically understated British fashion) that the move shocked her parents: "They were a bit disappointed he wasn't a homeowner and were certainly perplexed."[23]

Materialists are more likely to value possessions for their status and appearance-related meanings, whereas those who do not emphasize this value tend to prize products that connect them to other people or that provide them with pleasure in using them. As a result, high materialists prefer products likely to be publicly consumed and to be more expensive. A study that compared specific items that low versus high materialists value found that people low on the materialism value cherished items such as a mother's wedding gown, picture albums, a rocking chair from childhood, or a garden, whereas those who scored high preferred things such as jewelry, china, or a vacation home.[24]

U.S. society is struggling to reconcile desires for material goods with the need for environmental consciousness and spirituality. This shift is blurring some of the expected boundaries between

U.S. society is struggling to reconcile desires for material goods with the need for environmental consciousness and spirituality.

"traditional" and "progressive" segments. As one analyst noted, for example, even conservative small towns now often feature "new age" stores and services where people of all ages shop. Retailers that used to be considered "Bohemian" now are mainstream; grocers such as Fresh Fields sell Mayan Fungus soap and vegetarian dog biscuits to a hodgepodge of consumers. Big corporations such as Apple and The Gap use countercultural figures such as Gandhi and Jack Kerouac in their advertising, and Ben & Jerry's boasts of its unconventional corporate philosophy. It's become hard to separate establishment from antiestablishment as Bohemian attitudes of the hippie 1960s have merged with the bourgeois attitudes of the yuppie 1980s to form a new culture that is a synthesis of the two. The people who dominate our culture (this analyst calls them "BoBos," or *Bourgeois Bohemians*) now are richer and more worldly than hippies but more spiritual than yuppies.[25] Even core values change over time; stay tuned to see how our always-evolving culture continues to put a fresh spin on materialism and other values.

TRUTH

11

Your customers are looking for greener pastures

Are U.S. consumers finally going green—for real? In a 2007 survey, fully eight in ten consumers said they believe it's important to buy green brands and products from green companies, and that they'll pay more to do so. The U.S. consumer's focus on personal health is merging with a growing interest in global health. Some analysts call this new value *conscientious consumerism*.[26]

Just who is driving this change? Marketers point to a segment of consumers who practice LOHAS, an acronym for "lifestyles of health and sustainability." This label refers to people who worry about the environment, want products to be produced in a sustainable way, and who spend money to advance what they see as their personal development and potential. These "Lohasians" (others refer to this segment as *cultural creatives*) represent a great market for products such as organic foods, energy-efficient appliances, and hybrid cars, as well as alternative medicine, yoga tapes, and eco-tourism. One organization that tracks this group estimates they make up about 16 percent of the adults in the United States; it values the market for socially conscious products at more than $200 billion.[27]

Marketers and retailers are responding with thousands of new eco-friendly products. Colgate bought a big stake in the natural toothpaste brand Tom's of Maine, and L'Oréal acquired The Body Shop. Kellogg's introduced organic versions of some of its bestselling cereals.

Whereas in the past it was sufficient for companies to offer recyclable products, this new movement is creating a whole new vocabulary as consumers begin to "vote with their forks" by demanding food, fragrances, and other items that are made without genetically modified ingredients (GMOs), are hormone-free, don't involve animal clones or animal testing, are locally grown, and are cage-free, just to name a few of consumers' concerns and requirements. Indeed, between 2005 and 2006, grocery sales of products making ethical claims grew by 17 percent to nearly $33 billion. The food industry predicts sales of $57 billion by 2011.[28]

Although Lohasians have been fueling demand for eco-friendly products for several years, the big news today is that conscientious consumerism now is spreading to the mass market as well. In fact, even Wal-Mart is making the effort to go green. The world's largest retailer developed a survey called the "Live Better Index" that allows it to monitor customers' feelings about eco-friendly products. The first wave of research polled more than 2,500 Americans on five products: compact florescent light bulbs (CFLs), organic milk, concentrated/reduced-packaging liquid laundry detergents, extended-life paper products, and

The big news today is that conscientious consumerism now is spreading to the mass market.

organic baby food. In this survey, 62 percent of respondents said they would buy more eco-friendly products if there were no price difference. Nearly half (47 percent) said they completely agree that buying environmentally friendly products makes them feel like smart consumers, and 68 percent agree that "even the small act of recycling at home has an impact on the environment."[29]

As mainstream marketers recognize this change, they are starting to alter their practices to satisfy Americans' desires for healthy and earth-friendly products. Here are some recent examples.

- Home Depot, the nation's second-largest retailer, introduced an Eco Options label for almost 3,000 products, such as fluorescent light bulbs that conserve electricity and natural insect killers that promote energy conservation, sustainable forestry, and clean water. The company expects products it certifies under this program to represent 12 percent of its total sales by 2009.

- H&M is selling clothes made from organic cotton fabrics to fashion-conscious shoppers. Gap introduced an organic cotton T-shirt for men in more than 500 of its stores.

- Procter & Gamble Co. reduced the size of its packaging for its liquid detergent. It's switching to a double concentrate formula to serve its $4 billion North American liquid detergent market.

- Scotts' Organic Choice brand is part of the giant gardening company's move toward less dependence on synthetically created chemicals, which include the main components in its distinctive blue Miracle-Gro plant food.

Not content to wait for companies to change their practices, everyday consumers also are taking action. Many are joining organizations such as Slow Food to advocate for lifestyle changes. One such movement called "Local First" stresses the value of buying locally made products. This group (some members call themselves "locavores") values small community businesses, but it formed as a reaction to waste that results from people importing things they need from long distances. One proponent of this movement calculates that the average U.S. meal travels 1,500 miles before it lands on our dinner plates. This cause already is affecting the grocery industry; the U.S. Department of Agriculture reports that the number of farmers markets grew from 1,755 in 1994 to 4,388 in 2006. The popular Whole Foods chain recently tightened up its definition of local, using the label only if products traveled less than 7 hours from farm to store.

Still other consumers are rebelling against the huge market for bottled water. They object to the fact that some brands come from as far away as Fiji. These imports contribute to the creation of pollution because of the tanker ships that cart them halfway around the world and the waste that millions of discarded plastic bottles create. In the summer of 2007, San Francisco's mayor decreed that city government would not use city money to buy bottled water for its employees.

The environmental effect of an object seemingly as innocent as a plastic water bottle points to the concern many now have about the size of a product's *carbon footprint*; this measures, in units of carbon dioxide, the impact that human activities have on the environment in terms of the amount of greenhouse gases they produce. The average American is responsible for 9.44 tons of CO_2 per year![30]

Thousands of consumers use services such as Climate Clean and TerraPass that sell them *greenhouse gas (GHG) offsets.* These businesses enable individuals and businesses to reduce their GHG emissions by offsetting, reducing, or displacing the GHG to another place, typically where it is more economical to do so. Whether you're concerned (yet) about global warming, expect to see your business engulfed by a tidal wave of consumer interest in products that reduce our carbon footprint.

> Expect to see your business engulfed by a tidal wave of consumer interest in products that reduce our carbon footprint.

TRUTH

12

"Because I'm worth it"

When Sara Lee developed a new line of snack cakes, the company discovered that consumers with low self-esteem preferred portion-controlled snack items because they felt they lacked self-control. Self-esteem refers to the positivity of a person's self-concept. People with low self-esteem expect that they will not perform very well, and they will try to avoid embarrassment, failure, or rejection. Most of us don't seem to have that problem. We believe we deserve good things, and we want them now.

Alberto-Culver uses a self-esteem appeal to promote a new product that reflects our changing society: Soft & Beautiful Just for Me Texture Softener, an alternative to hair pressing or relaxing. It's targeted to white mothers who don't know how to care for the hair of their multiracial children who have "hair texture" issues. The self-esteem portion of the campaign, dubbed "Love Yourself. Love Your Hair," includes a Web site, texturesoftener.com, that offers "conversation starters" to help parents find ways to talk to their daughters about self-image.

> We believe we deserve good things, and we want them now.

Indeed, many people must have really strong egos these days to judge by the bravado they display in offering themselves up for inspection on the Web. Millions have posted their photos to be rated by visitors to hotornot.com, a hot Web site where visitors rate each picture on a scale from 1 to 10. One of the site's two creators remembers, "Basically, we were sitting around drinking beers in the middle of the afternoon when a comment Jim made about a woman he had seen at a party made us think, wouldn't it be cool if there was a Web site where you could tell if a girl was a perfect 10?" The phenomenal success of the site spawned hundreds of copycats, many of them not exactly the PG-rated environment that this site offers. Some of the photos people send in aren't what you would call flattering (especially the ones submitted as jokes on unsuspecting friends); one possible explanation is the psychological concept of self-handicapping, where we set ourselves up for failure so that, in case ratings are low, we can blame the picture rather than ourselves. Another is that the world is crowded with people so hungry for attention that they will submit to any number of indignities to have others look at them.[31]

Marketing communications can influence a consumer's self-esteem. Exposure to ads portraying (often unrealistic) buff men and svelte women can trigger a process of *social comparison*, where the person tries to evaluate herself by comparing it to the people these artificial images depict. This act of evaluating is a basic human

> Many marketers tap into our need for benchmarks by supplying idealized images of happy, attractive people who just happen to be using their products.

tendency, and many marketers tap into our need for benchmarks by supplying idealized images of happy, attractive people who just happen to be using their products. A recent ad campaign for Clearasil is a good example. In one typical ad, two teenage boys enter a kitchen where a 40-ish mother is mixing something in a bowl. When her son leaves the room, his friend hits on Mom. The ad's tagline: "Clearasil may cause confidence."

A study that illustrates the social comparison process showed that female college students tend to compare their physical appearance with models in advertising. Furthermore, study participants who were exposed to beautiful women in advertisements afterward expressed lowered satisfaction with their own appearance, as compared to other participants who did not view ads with attractive models.[32] Another study demonstrated that young women alter their perceptions of their own body shapes and sizes after they watch as little as 30 minutes of TV programming.[33] Researchers report similar findings for men.[34]

Self-esteem advertising attempts to change our attitudes toward products by stimulating positive feelings about the self. One strategy is to challenge the consumer's self-esteem and then show a linkage to a product that provides a remedy. For example, the Marine Corps uses this strategy with its theme "If you have what it takes...." Another strategy is outright flattery, as when Virginia Slims cigarette ads proclaim, "You've come a long way, baby."

TRUTH

13

Love me, love my avatar

In the influential cyberpunk novel *Snow Crash*, author Neal Stephenson envisioned a virtual world, called the Metaverse, as a successor to the Internet. In the Metaverse, everyday people take on glamorous identities in a three-dimensional immersive digital world. The book's main character delivers pizza in real life, but in the Metaverse, he's a warrior prince and champion sword fighter. The hugely popular *Matrix* movie trilogy paints a similar (though more sinister) picture of a world that blurs the lines between physical and digital reality.

Today, these fictional depictions come to life as we witness the tremendous growth of real-time, interactive virtual worlds that allow people to assume virtual identities in cyberspace. More than nine million people worldwide belong to the virtual world of *Second Life*, more than eight million play the online game *World of Warcraft*, and one-third of Korean adults socialize in CyWorld. Add to that the millions more who play *The Sims Online* or who visit other computer-mediated environments (CMEs) such as Webkinz, There, Whyville, Entropia Universe, MTV's Virtual Laguna Beach, and so on, and you're looking at a lot of serious role-playing.

> People assume visual identities, or avatars, ranging from realistic versions of themselves to tricked-out versions with "exaggerated" physical characteristics or winged dragons or superheroes.

On these sites, people assume visual identities, or *avatars*, ranging from realistic versions of themselves to tricked-out versions with "exaggerated" physical characteristics or winged dragons or superheroes. Researchers are just starting to investigate how these online selves will influence consumer behavior and how the identities we choose in CMEs relate to our real life (RL) or "meat-world" identities. Already we know that when people take on avatar forms, they tend to interact with other avatars much as their meat-world selves interact with other RL people. For example, just as in the RL, males in *Second Life* leave more space between them when talking to other males versus females, and they are less likely to maintain eye contact than are females. And when avatars get very close to one another, they tend to look away from each other. The norms of the RL are creeping into the virtual world.

You heard it here first: Virtual worlds will be the next huge marketing platform.

If you don't know it already, you heard it here first: Virtual worlds will be the next huge marketing platform. Don't miss the (virtual) boat on this one!

TRUTH

14

You really are
what you wear

Some stores are testing a new interactive mirror that doubles as a high-resolution digital screen. When you choose an article of clothing, the mirror superimposes it on your reflection so that you can see how it would look on you. A camera relays live images of you modeling your virtual outfit to an Internet site where your friends can log to instant message (IM) you to tell you what they think; their comments pop up on the side of the mirror for you to read. They can also select virtual items for you to try on that will be reflected in the "magic" mirror.

Sociologists call the process of imagining the reactions of others toward us "taking the role of the other," or the *looking-glass self*. According to this view, our desire to define ourselves operates as a sort of psychological sonar: We take readings of our own identity by "bouncing" signals off others and trying to project the impression they have of us. Of course, like the distorted mirrors in a funhouse, our appraisal of who we are varies depending on whose perspective we consider and how accurately we predict their evaluations of us.

How does this process impact on the bottom line? Plenty. Since the reflection we see in this psychological mirror includes the products we are wearing, driving, eating, and so on, it follows that customers' identities reflect what they choose to buy from you (or from your competitors). In fact, in our consumption-oriented society, people increasingly bond with favorite products—to the extent that they may literally become walking billboards that promote their choices to others. *Identity marketing* is a promotional strategy where consumers alter some aspects of their selves to advertise for a branded product. For example, The Internet Underground Music Archive (IUMA) paid a Kansas couple $5,000 to name their baby boy Iuma. The Daytona Cubs baseball team awards free season tickets for life to anyone who will tattoo the Cubs logo on their body. Play ball!

> Customers' identities reflect what they choose to buy from you (or from your competitors).

Our use of consumption information to define the self is especially important when we have yet to totally form a social identity, such as when we find ourselves playing a new role in life. Think, for example, of the insecurity many of us felt when we first started college or reentered the dating market after leaving a really long relationship. *Symbolic self-completion theory* suggests that people who have an incomplete self-definition tend to complete this identity by acquiring and displaying symbols they associate with that role. As we mature into a role, we actually rely less on the products people associate with it. For example, when kids start to skateboard, they often invest in pro skateboard "decks" with graphics and branding that cost between $40 and $70 even without the "trucks" (wheels and axles). But—to the chagrin of the skateboard industry—as kids get more serious about boarding, many think it's just fine to buy "blank decks"; the plain wood boards cost only $15 to $30.

Because many consumption activities are related to self-definition, it is not surprising to learn that consumers demonstrate consistency between their values and the things they buy, including products such as beer, soap, toothpaste, and cigarettes relative to their least preferred brands, as well as between their self-images and their favorite stores. One of the earliest studies to examine this process found that car owners' ratings of themselves tended to match their perceptions of their cars: Pontiac drivers saw themselves as more active and flashy than did Volkswagen drivers.[35] Indeed, a recent German study found that observers were able to match photos of male and female drivers to pictures of the cars they drove almost 70 percent of the time.[36]

The external objects that we consider a part of us comprise what researchers call the *extended self*. In some cultures, people literally incorporate objects into the self—they lick new possessions, take the names of conquered enemies (or in some cases eat them), or bury the dead with their possessions. We don't usually go that far, but some people do cherish possessions as if they were a part of them.

Consider shoes, for example. You don't have to be Carrie of *Sex and the City* fame to acknowledge that many people feel a strong bond to their footwear. One study found that people commonly view their shoes as magical emblems of self—Cinderella-like vehicles for self-transformation.[37] In addition to shoes, of course, many material objects ranging from personal possessions and pets to national monuments or landmarks help to form a consumer's identity. Just about everyone can name a valued possession that has a lot of the self "wrapped up" in it, whether it is a beloved photograph, a trophy, an old shirt, a car, or a cat. Indeed, usually we can construct a pretty accurate "biography" of someone simply by cataloging the items on display in his bedroom or office. Clothes (and many other products) do make the man.

Clothes (and many other products) do make the man.

TRUTH

15

Real men don't eat quiche
(but they do moisturize)

Sony created a TV ad for its Bravia line of liquid-crystal-display (LCD) televisions that offers different endings to men and women. The spot shows a man and a woman gazing through a storefront window at a Bravia LCD. Unaware of each other, the two simultaneously whisper: "Nice picture." Suddenly, two buttons appear on the screen that read: "Ending for Men" and "Ending for Women." The male ending is either a funny clip from a sports show or a cartoon spoof of a martial-arts movie. Women see either a 1950s-era musical centered on shoes or a tear-jerker about a female doctor who saves the life of an orphan.

Sexual identity is an important component of a consumer's self-concept. People often conform to their culture's expectations about how those of their gender should act, dress, or speak. Of course, these guidelines change over time, and they differ radically across societies. It's unclear to what extent gender differences are innate versus culturally shaped—but they're certainly evident in many consumption situations.

Consider the gender differences that market researchers observe when they compare the food preferences of men to those of women. Women eat more fruit; men are more likely to eat meat. As one food writer put it, "Boy food doesn't grow. It is hunted or killed."[38] The sexes also differ sharply in the quantities of food they eat: When researchers at Hershey discovered that women eat smaller amounts of candy, they created a white chocolate confection called Hugs, one of the most successful food introductions of all time. However, a man in a Burger King Whopper ad ditches his date at a fancy restaurant, complaining that he is "too hungry to settle for chick food." Pumped up on Whoppers, a swelling mob of men shake their fists, punch one another, toss a van off a bridge, and sing, "I will eat this meat until my innie turns into an outie," and "I am hungry. I am incorrigible. I am man."

> Sexual identity is an important component of a consumer's self-concept.

Society sends mixed messages to men. Our culture's stereotype of the ideal male is a tough, aggressive, muscular man who enjoys "manly" sports (and *The Man Show* on Comedy Central). Just as for women, however, the true story is more complicated than that. One consequence is that men are concerned as never before with their appearance. Men spend $7.7 billion on grooming products globally each year.

Men are concerned as never before with their appearance.

Men are showing a willingness to use other traditionally feminine products, such as depilatories, to give them that smooth-torso look. They're even buying vanity products that alter their shape, including Bodyslimmers underwear that holds in the waist, Super Shaper Briefs that round out the buttocks, and the C-In2 "sling" brief that provides a lift similar to the Wonder Bra (along with a new version of this gravity-defying product called the Trophy Shelf).

No doubt one of the biggest marketing buzzwords over the past few years is the *metrosexual*, a straight, urban male who is keenly interested in fashion, home design, gourmet cooking, and personal care. A gay writer named Mark Simpson actually coined the term way back in a 1994 article when he "outed" British (and now American) soccer star and pop icon David Beckham as a metrosexual. Simpson noted that Beckham is "almost as famous for wearing sarongs and pink nail polish and panties belonging to his wife, Victoria (aka Posh from the Spice Girls), as he is for his impressive ball skills."[39]

Hype aside, how widespread is the metrosexual phenomenon? Although there's no doubt that "everyday guys" are expanding their horizons, many actively resist this label because they don't want others to question their sexual preferences. Clearly, our cultural definition of masculinity is evolving as men try to redefine sex roles while they stay in a "safety zone" of acceptable behaviors bounded by danger zones of sloppiness at one extreme and effeminate behavior at the other. For example, a man may decide that it's okay to use a moisturizer but draw the line at an eye cream that he considers too feminine. Some cultural observers even report the emergence of "retrosexuals;" men who want to emphasize their old-school masculinity by getting plastic surgery to create a more rugged look that includes hairier chests and beards, squarer chins, and more angular jaw lines.

Indeed, in many circles, the "M word" has become taboo and other (perhaps less threatening) labels are popping up instead. One such label is the übersexual, which *The Urban Dictionary* defines as

> metro-sexuality for the noughties (2000–2009)…. Übersexuals are the most attractive (not just physically), most dynamic, and most compelling men of their generations. They are confident, masculine, stylish, and committed to uncompromising quality in all areas of life…without giving into the negative stereotypes such as chauvinism, emotional unavailability, and a brain only filled with sports stats, beer, and burgers….

The current icon of übersexuals is Bono. He's global and socially aware, confident, and compassionate. Other notable übersexuals are Bill Clinton, George Clooney, Jon Stewart, Pierce Brosnan, Donald Trump, and Ewan McGregor.

Miller Genuine Draft recently conducted a survey of American men aged 21 to 34 to try to get a handle on these new definitions. The company found that, indeed, many "average Joes" are moving on from the days of drinking whatever beer is available and wearing baseball hats backward, but they also don't want to sacrifice their identities as regular guys. They care more about preparing a good meal, meeting friends for a beer, and owning a home than they do about amassing shoes, savoring fine wine, or dining at expensive restaurants. Indeed, 57 percent of men aged 25 to 29 say that if a woman were simply to pop in, they could whip up a full meal in a moment's notice with the items they have in the house.[40] The survey is silent about preferences for quiche.

TRUTH

16

Girls just want to have fun

In the 1949 movie *Adam's Rib*, Katherine Hepburn played a stylish and competent lawyer. This film was one of the first to show that a woman can have a successful career and still be happily married. Today, the evolution of a new managerial class of women has forced marketers to change their traditional assumptions about women as they target this growing market. For example, Suzuki is going out of its way to appeal to the growing number of women in India who are achieving financial independence and buying their own cars. Its Zen Estilo (Estilo means "style" in Spanish) model comes in eight colors, including purple fusion, virgin blue, and sparkling olive.

These changes have forced marketers to reexamine their strategies. For example, most sporting goods manufacturers have long sold products for women, but this often meant simply creating an inferior version of the male product and slapping a pink label on it. Then the companies discovered that many women were buying products intended for boys because they wanted better quality, so some of them figured out that they needed to take this market segment seriously. Burton Snowboard Company was one of the early learners. When the company started to offer high-quality clothing and gear made specifically for women, female boarders snapped them up. Burton also changed the way it promoted these products. It redesigned its Web site after getting feedback from female riders. Now, models in the women's section are shot from the bottom looking up, which makes them look more empowered. In contrast, the photos in the men's section feature tighter shots of the gear itself, since Burton's research showed that males are more interested in the technical details.

Some smart marketers have figured out that products men traditionally love appeal to women as well. In the automotive industry, they are discovering that a growing number of women spend big bucks to add extra horsepower to their cars, along with 17-inch wheels, custom racing seats, and

> Smart marketers have figured out that products men traditionally love appeal to women as well.

other accessories. Although attributes such as safety, security, and reliability still appeal to women, like men they are increasingly drawn to power, speed, and hot looks. The so-called tuner industry, which includes aftermarket products such as spoilers, Xenon headlights, and turbochargers, is feeling this change—women now buy almost 25 percent of the $2.2 billion in merchandise and services that car freaks purchase each year.

Similarly, the high-tech industry launched a "Technology is a girl's best friend" campaign to entice women to buy more electronics products. This makes sense, because the Consumer Electronics Association estimates that about 75 percent of consumer-electronics purchasing decisions involve women. Gateway even managed to get a pink laptop computer prominently placed in the movie *Legally Blonde 2*. Other manufacturers are coming out with

The Consumer Electronics Association estimates that about 75 percent of consumer-electronics purchasing decisions involve women.

products ranging from headphones to cell phone covers in pink and other feminine colors to attract women. Palm's Zire Handheld PDA emphasizes its clear packaging and simple name. Palm's new focus evidently worked: For the first time with any Palm product, more than half of Zire buyers are women.

And women are invading that bastion of maleness we call video games. They make up about 40 percent of the total gaming audience. Some 64 percent of online gamers in the United States are female according to a recent Nielsen study. And in the emerging mobile-game market, women account for 55 percent of players. For example, Buena Vista Games targets women aged 18 to 49 with a PC game based on *Desperate Housewives*.

Sex roles constantly evolve. In a complex society like ours, we often encounter contradictory messages about "appropriate" behavior. We can clearly see this in the messages girls have been getting from the media for the past several years: It's cool to be slutty. Role models

Is our culture moving from a celebration of "girls gone wild" to "girls gone mild"?

like Paris Hilton, Lindsay Lohan, Britney Spears, and even Bratz dolls convey standards about how far preteens and teens should go in broadcasting their sexuality. Now, as these messages seem to go over the top (at least in the eyes of some concerned parents), we start to see early signs of a backlash. At the Pure Fashion Web site, girls get style tips including skirts and dresses that fall no more than four fingers above the knee and no tank tops without a sweater or jacket over them. Several other sites, such as ModestApparelUSA.com and ModestByDesign.com, advocate a return to styles that leave almost everything to the imagination. Is our culture moving from a celebration of "girls gone wild" to "girls gone mild"?

TRUTH
17

Queer eye for the
spending guy

Mars aired a commercial during the 2007 Super Bowl that stirred up a lot of controversy. Eventually, the company agreed to stop airing the ad after organizations such as the Gay and Lesbian Alliance against Defamation protested. The ad shows two mechanics eating from opposite ends of a Snickers candy bar until their lips touch. Shocked and dismayed by this linkup, they rip out their chest hair in a desperate attempt to "do something manly."

Mars probably managed to insult more consumers than the company realizes. The proportion of the population that is gay or lesbian is difficult to determine, and efforts to measure this group have been controversial. The respected research company Yankelovich Partners Inc., which has tracked consumer values and attitudes since 1971 in its annual Monitor survey, now includes a question about sexual identity in its instrument and reports that about 6 percent of respondents identify themselves as gay/homosexual/lesbian. This study was virtually the first to use a sample that reflects the population as a whole instead of polling only smaller or biased groups (such as readers of gay publications) whose responses may not be as representative of all consumers.

These results help to paint a more accurate picture of the potential size and attractiveness of the Gay, Lesbian, Bisexual, and Transgendered (GLBT) market segment. To put things in perspective, the GLBT market is at least as large, if not larger, than the Asian American population (currently at about 12 million people). These consumers spend in the range of $250 billion to $350 billion a year. A Simmons study of readers of gay publications found that readers are almost 12 times more likely to hold professional jobs, twice as likely to own a vacation home, and eight times more likely to own a notebook computer compared to heterosexuals.

In the mid-1990s, IKEA, a Swedish furniture retailer with stores in several major U.S. markets, broke new ground by running a TV spot featuring a gay couple that purchased a dining room table at the store. For many consumers,

The GLBT market is at least as large, if not larger, than the Asian American population.

gay culture is more familiar largely because of the prominence of gay people in popular shows such as *The L Word* and because of decisions by stars such as Ellen DeGeneres and Rosie O'Donnell to openly discuss their sexuality.

Also, although it has been common for years for these companies to run ads in gay publications (often unbeknown to their straight customers), now major marketers, including American Express, Audi, Cartier, Chili's, Diageo, Marshall Field's, General Motors, Target, Volkswagen, and Wrigley, are using openly gay and lesbian celebrities in campaigns aimed at the wider general audience. They are hiring personalities such as singers k.d. lang and Melissa Etheridge; designers Isaac Mizrahi and Todd Oldham; actor John Cameron Mitchell; and John Amaechi, a former NBA center and the first professional basketball player to disclose that he is gay.

American Express, Stolichnaya vodka, Atlantic Records, and Naya bottled water are among those corporations that run ads in lesbian publications (an ad for American Express Travelers Cheques for Two shows two women's signatures on a check). Acting on research that showed lesbians are four times as likely as the average consumer to own one of their cars, Subaru of America decided to target this market in a big way. And in one of the first mainstream pitches to directly address the controversy over gay marriage, Grand Marnier, a French cognac, launched print ads that read, "Your sister is finally getting remarried. Her fiancée's name is Jill."

> Major marketers are using openly gay and lesbian celebrities in campaigns aimed at the wider general audience.

Don't ignore the vast spending power of this consumer segment. As the saying goes, "We're here, we're queer, and we're going shopping."

TRUTH

18

Yesterday's chubby is
today's voluptuous

The size and shape of the "average" U.S. consumer today is dramatically different from what it was 60 years ago. Nevertheless, apparel companies still develop clothing lines based on a 1941 military study that set sizing standards based on a small sample of mostly white, young (and presumably physically fit) female soldiers. Those standards are finally starting to change based on the fact that the typical woman's body is no longer as "petite" as it used to be. The most commonly purchased dress today is a size 14; it was a size 8 in 1985!

Standards based upon an outdated snapshot of U.S. women need to recognize the diversity of today's ethnic population: According to current criteria, fully 78 percent of African American women and 72 percent of Hispanic women are overweight, compared to 58 percent of white women. And non-Caucasian body shapes differ as well—for example, Hispanic Americans and Asian Americans tend to be shorter than their Caucasian counterparts. The clothing industry can't take the market potential of this segment lightly—women spent about $47 billion on plus-size garments in 2005, accounting for 20 percent of the total apparel market.

The standards we use to evaluate physical attractiveness go more than skin deep. Beauty affects a wide range of outcomes, as we *do* tend to judge a book by its cover. By the way, this bias affects both men and women—men with above-average looks earn about five percent more than those of average appearance, and those who are below average in appearance make an average of nine percent less than the norm.

Standards based upon an outdated snapshot of U.S. women need to recognize the diversity of today's ethnic population.

Although beauty may be only skin deep, throughout history women have worked hard to attain it. They have starved themselves; painfully bound their feet; inserted plates into their lips; spent countless hours under hair dryers, in front of mirrors, and beneath tanning lights; and opted for breast reduction or enlargement operations to alter their appearance and meet their society's expectations of what a beautiful woman should look like.

In retrospect, we can characterize periods of history by a specific "look," or ideal of beauty. Often these relate to broader cultural happenings, such as today's

> Beauty affects a wide range of outcomes, as we *do* tend to judge a book by its cover.

emphasis on fitness and toned bodies. One study compared measures of the public's favorite actresses with socioeconomic indicators between 1932 and 1995. When market conditions were bad, people preferred actresses with mature features, including small eyes, thin cheeks, and a large chin. When the economy was in good shape, however, the public embraced women with babyish features, such as large eyes and full cheeks.

In much of the nineteenth century, the desirable waistline for U.S. women was 18 inches, a circumference that required the use of corsets pulled so tight that they routinely caused headaches, fainting spells, and possibly even the uterine and spinal disorders common among women of the time. Although modern women are not quite as "straight-laced," many still endure such indignities as high heels, body waxing, eyelifts, and liposuction. In addition to the millions women spend on cosmetics, clothing, health clubs, and fashion magazines, these practices remind us that—rightly or wrongly—the desire to conform to current standards of beauty is alive and well.

Our culture communicates these standards—subtly and not so subtly—virtually everywhere we turn: on magazine covers, in department store windows, on TV shows. Feminists argue that fashion dolls, such as the ubiquitous Barbie, reinforce an unnatural ideal of thinness. When we extrapolate the dimensions of these dolls to average female body sizes, indeed they are unnaturally long and thin. If the traditional Barbie doll were a real woman, her dimensions would be 38-18-34! In 1998, Mattel conducted "plastic surgery" on Barbie to give her a less pronounced bust and slimmer hips, but she is still not exactly dumpy.

A provocative campaign by Dove that started in Europe featuring women with imperfect bodies in their underwear may help. One ad reads, "Let's face it, firming the thighs of a size 8 supermodel wouldn't have been much of a challenge." Unilever initiated the campaign after its research showed that many women didn't believe its products worked because the women shown using them were so unrealistic. Perhaps at least partly because of the success of the Dove campaign, other companies also are turning to ordinary people instead of professional models when they advertise. McDonald's held a casting call for consumers who will appear on its world cup and bag packaging as an extension of its "I'm lovin' it" campaign. Nike and Wal-Mart also have run advertisements with average Janes.

Will the backlash against the pressure to be thin reach the more rarefied air of the *haute couture* industry, whose customers can never (as the saying goes) be too thin or too rich? A few recent tragedies have certainly fueled the fire; in less than two months, four young Brazilian women died in widely publicized cases of anorexia, which sparked an international debate about body image and eating disorders. Unilever banned the use of so-called "size 0" models in its ads for products ranging from Lux shower gel and Sunsilk shampoo to Slim-Fast diet drinks. How permanent will these changes be? For now, we'll simply have to weight and see.

TRUTH

19

Men want to sleep with their cars

Consider the case of a Tennessee man who tried to marry his car. His plan was thwarted after he listed his fiancée's birthplace as Detroit, her father as Henry Ford, and her blood type as 10W40. Under Tennessee law, only a man and a woman can legally wed.

His attachment may be a bit extreme (or so we hope), but there's no doubt that cars function as sexual surrogates. This example underscores the ways that some of our possessions "speak" to us. In fact, these relationships start to look positively Freudian...Sigmund Freud proposed that much of one's adult personality stems from a fundamental conflict between a desire to gratify physical needs and the necessity to function as a responsible member of society. Perhaps products like red convertibles provide an outlet to do just that.

> There's no doubt that cars function as sexual surrogates.

Back in the 1950s, a school of thought called motivational research started to borrow Freudian ideas to understand the deeper meanings of products and advertisements. This approach adapted psychoanalytical (Freudian) interpretations with a heavy emphasis on unconscious motives. It basically assumed that we channel socially unacceptable needs into acceptable outlets—including product substitutes.

Ernest Dichter, a psychoanalyst who trained in Vienna in the early part of the twentieth century, pioneered this work. Dichter conducted in-depth interview studies on more than 230 different products, and actual marketing campaigns incorporated many of his findings. For example, Esso (now Exxon in the United States) for many years reminded consumers to "Put a Tiger in Your Tank" after Dichter found that people responded well to this powerful animal symbolism containing vaguely sexual undertones. These are some other insights that surfaced from this research:

■ Women equate the act of baking a cake from scratch with giving birth. Instant cake mixes didn't sell well when they were introduced; they did better when they were reformulated to require the cook to break an egg into the mix.

■ Men are reluctant to donate blood because they fear their "vital fluids" will be depleted. The Red Cross addressed this fear with the slogan, "Give the gift of life" so that men would feel they were (symbolically) fertilizing others rather than being drained.

■ Men feel secure if they have a full drawer of neatly ironed shirts or folded socks.

■ White bread, cotton fabrics, and harsh household cleaning chemicals connote moral purity and cleanliness.

■ Kitchen appliances, boats, sporting goods, and cigarette lighters convey mastery over the environment.

■ Soups have magical healing powers, and carbonated drinks possess a magical effervescent property.

■ Houses with large doorknobs will sell better because they subconsciously remind prospective buyers of how the entrance to their own home felt when they were little and had tiny hands.

Although this Freudian perspective has not been in vogue among researchers for quite some time, the basic notion that marketers need to understand the "deep meanings" of products that go well beyond their basic functions is alive and well. For example, Carl Jung, another of Freud's disciples, continues to influence some advertisers' strategies (including the major ad agency Young & Rubicam). Freud was grooming Jung to be his successor, but his protégé was unable to accept Freud's emphasis on sexual aspects of personality, and the two men went their separate ways. Jung went on to develop his own method of psychotherapy he called *analytical psychology*.

Jung believed that the cumulative experiences of past generations shape who we are today. He proposed that we each share a *collective unconscious*—a storehouse of memories that we inherit from our ancestors. For example, Jung would argue that many people are afraid of the dark because their distant ancestors had good reason

These shared
memories create
archetypes,
or universally
recognized ideas
and behavior
patterns. These
images appear
frequently
in marketing
messages that use
characters such as
wizards, revered
teachers, or even
Mother Nature.

to fear it. These shared memories create archetypes, or universally recognized ideas and behavior patterns. Archetypes involve themes, such as birth, death, or the devil, that appear frequently in myths, stories, and dreams.

Jung's ideas may seem a bit far-fetched, but advertising messages, in fact, do often include archetypes. For example, two that Jung and his followers identified are the "old wise man" and the "earth mother." These images appear frequently in marketing messages that use characters such as wizards, revered teachers, or even Mother Nature. Our culture's infatuation with stories such as *Harry Potter* and *The Lord of the Rings* speaks to the power of these images.

TRUTH

20

Your PC is trying to kill you

In 1886, a momentous event occurred in marketing history—the Quaker Oats man first appeared on boxes of hot cereal. Quakers had a reputation in nineteenth-century America for being shrewd but fair, and peddlers sometimes dressed as members of this religious group to cash in on their credibility. When the cereal company decided to "borrow" this imagery for its packaging, this signaled the recognition that its customers might make the same association.

Today, thousands of brands borrow personality traits of individuals or groups to convey an image they want customers to form of them. A brand personality is the set of traits people attribute to a product as if it were a person. Many of the most recognizable figures in popular culture are spokescharacters for long-standing brands, such as the Jolly Green Giant, the Keebler Elves, Mr. Peanut, and Charlie the Tuna.

Our feelings about a brand's personality are part of brand equity, which refers to the extent to which a consumer holds strong, favorable, and unique associations with a brand in memory—and the extent to which she or he is willing to pay more for the branded version of a product than for a nonbranded (generic) version. Building strong brands is good business. If you don't believe it, consider that, in a study of 760 Fortune 1,000 companies after the stock market took a nosedive in October of 1997, the 20 strongest corporate brands (for example, Microsoft and GE) actually gained in market value, whereas the 20 weakest lost an average of $1 billion each.[41]

Brands borrow personality traits of individuals or groups to convey an image they want customers to form of them.

An advertising agency wrote the following memo to help it figure out how to portray one of its clients. Based on this description of the "client," can you guess who he is? "He is creative...unpredictable...an imp.... He not only walks and talks, but also has the ability to sing, blush, wink, and work with little devices like pointers.... He can also play musical instruments.... His walking motion is characterized as a 'swagger.'.... He is made of dough and has mass." Of course, we all know today that packaging and other physical cues create a "personality" for a product (in this case, the Pillsbury Doughboy).

A product that creates and communicates a distinctive brand personality stands out from its competition and inspires years of loyalty. However, personality analysis helps marketers identify a brand's weaknesses that have little to do with its functional qualities. adidas asked kids in focus groups to imagine that the brand came to life and was at a party, and to tell what they would expect the brand to be doing there. The kids responded that adidas would be hanging around the keg with its pals, talking about girls. Unfortunately, they also said Nike would be *with* the girls!"[42] These results reminded adidas' brand managers that they had some work to do. We compare this process to animism, the common cultural practice whereby people give inanimate objects qualities that make them somehow alive.

A brand's positioning strategy is a statement about what that brand wants to be in the eyes of its customers—especially relative to the competition. Marketers typically think in these terms (even if they haven't read this book); they routinely describe their brands and the competition as if they were people. For example, here's how the marketing director for Philips Electronics in Asia sums up the problem he faces in updating his brand so that it's seen as hip and young by Chinese consumers: "To put it bluntly, we are received well by middle-aged gentlemen…. But a brand like Sony is seen as younger, more arrogant, with a space-age personality."[43]

> Brands personality is a statement about the brand's market position.

In a sense, then, a brand personality is a statement about the brand's market position. Understanding this is crucial to marketing strategy, especially if consumers don't see the brand the way its makers intend them to and they must attempt to reposition the product (give it a personality makeover). That's the problem Volvo now faces; its cars are renowned for safety, but drivers don't exactly see them as exciting or sexy. A safe and solid brand personality makes it hard to sell a racy convertible like the C70 model, so a

British ad tries to change that perception with the tagline, "Lust, envy, jealousy. The dangers of a Volvo." Just as with people, however, you can only go so far to convince others that your personality has changed. Volvo has been trying to jazz up its image for years, but for the most part consumers aren't buying it. In an earlier attempt in the United Kingdom, the company paired action images like a Volvo pulling a helicopter off a cliff with the headline "Safe Sex"—but market research showed people didn't believe the new image. As one brand consultant observed, "You get the sort of feeling you get when you see your grandparents trying to dance the latest dance. Slightly amused and embarrassed."[44]

TRUTH

21

Birds of a feather
buy together

Nike makes a lot of shoes and athletic apparel, but now the company wants to play an even bigger role in your daily life. It commissioned original workout music for its "Nike + Original Run" series that you can buy at Apple's iTunes Music Store. It teamed up with Apple to offer the Nike + shoes that feature a built-in pocket under the insole for the Nike + iPod sensor that lets you track your run and set goals while listening to your favorite tunes. It's releasing other CDs featuring music and voice-over coaching in activities such as yoga, dance, and weight training.

In traditional societies, class, caste, village, or family largely dictate a person's consumption options. In a modern consumer society, however, people are freer to select the set of products, services, and activities that define themselves and, in turn, create a social identity they communicate to others. One's choice of goods and services (do you choose to "just do it" with Nike?) makes a statement about who one is and about the types of people with whom one desires to identify—and even those whom we wish to avoid.

A lifestyle marketing perspective recognizes that people sort themselves into groups on the basis of the things they like to do, how they like to spend their leisure time, and how they choose to spend their disposable income. The growing number of niche magazines that cater to specialized interests reflects the rainbow of choices available to us in today's society. In one recent year, *WWF Magazine* (World Wrestling Federation) gained 913,000 readers, and *4 Wheel & Off Road* gained 749,000, whereas mainstream *Reader's Digest* lost more than 3 million readers, and *People* lost more than 2 million.

> Brand personality is a statement about the brand's market position and makes a statement about who one is and about the types of people with whom one desires to identify—and even those whom we wish to avoid.

These finely tuned choices, in turn, create opportunities for market segmentation strategies that recognize the potency of a consumer's chosen lifestyle in determining both the types of products purchased and the specific brands most likely to appeal to a certain lifestyle segment. For example, the popularity of wrestling is creating other lifestyle marketing opportunities. The WWE (World Wrestling Entertainment) is lending its name to the Socko Energy line of beverages that Wal-Mart sells. The drinks include "WWE Slammin' Citrus Powered by Socko" and "WWE Raw Attitude Powered by Socko." In turn, Bliss Beverages, which makes the beverages, will sponsor WWE pay-per-view matches. Now that's opening a can of lifestyle marketing Whoop-ass!

Marketers often find it useful to develop products that appeal to different lifestyle groups. Simply knowing a person's income doesn't predict whether he will drive a Cadillac Escalade SUV pickup or a Cadillac El Dorado sedan. To do this, they need a way to "breathe life" into demographic data to identify, understand, and target consumer segments that will share a set of preferences for their products and services. When they combine personality variables with knowledge of lifestyle preferences, they have a powerful lens they can focus on consumer segments. We call this approach *psychographics*. Adidas, for example, describes different types of shoe buyers in terms of lifestyles so that it can address the needs of segments, such as *gearheads* (hard-core, older runners who want high-performance shoes), *popgirls* (teeny-boppers who hang out at the mall and wear Skechers), and fastidious *eclectus* (Bohemian, cutting-edge types who want hip, distinctive products).

Most contemporary psychographic research attempts to group consumers according to some combination of three categories of variables—activities, interests, and opinions—that we call AIOs. Using data from large samples, marketers create profiles of customers who resemble each other in terms of their activities and patterns of product usage. It's according to a general rule of thumb that marketers call this the 80/20 rule—only 20 percent of a product's users account for 80 percent of the volume of product a company sells. Researchers attempt to determine who uses the brand and try to isolate heavy, moderate, and light users.

The latest and hottest extension of lifestyle marketing is *behavioral targeting*, which refers to presenting people with advertisements based on their Internet use. Today, it's fairly easy for marketers to tailor the ads you see to Web sites you've visited. Some critics feel this is a mixed blessing, because it implies that big companies are tracking where we go and keeping this information.

Indeed, there are important privacy issues still to be resolved, but, interestingly, many consumers seem more than happy to trade off some of their personal information in exchange for information they consider more useful to them. A 2006 survey on this issue reported that 57 percent of the consumers it polled said they were willing to provide demographic information in exchange for a personalized online experience. And three-quarters of those involved in an online social network felt that this process would improve their experience because it would introduce them to others who shared their tastes and interests. However, a majority still expressed concern about the security of their personal data online.[45]

Pro or con, it's clear that behavioral targeting is starting to take off in a big way. For example, Blockbuster.com uses software that recommends videos to a customer based on attributes the flick shares with other movies she has already ordered. This results in some suggestions that may not be immediately obvious. Thus, someone who watched *Crash* might receive a recommendation for *Little Miss Sunshine* because both involve dysfunctional social groups, dynamic pacing, and an interdependent ensemble cast. Blockbuster says the service has increased its average customer's "to watch list" by almost 50 percent.

Behavioral targeting is starting to take off in a big way.

TRUTH

22

Sell wine spritzers to squash players

Because a goal of lifestyle marketing is to allow consumers to pursue their chosen ways to enjoy their lives and express their social identities, a key aspect of this strategy is to focus on product usage in desirable social settings. The desire to associate a product with a social situation is a long-standing one for advertisers, whether they include the product in a round of golf, a family barbecue, or a night at a glamorous club surrounded by the hip-hop elite.

We get a clearer picture of how people use products to define lifestyles when we see how they make choices in a variety of product categories. A lifestyle marketing perspective implies that we must look at *patterns of behavior* to understand consumers. Sadly, most marketers don't get this; they are so busy focusing on their immediate competitors within the same product space that they fail to understand how their brand "fits" into the consumer's broader pattern of consumption. They are missing out on a lot by looking too hard at a few trees instead of surveying the entire forest!

> A lifestyle marketing perspective implies that we must look at *patterns of behavior* to understand consumers.

When we do take the forest view, we quickly realize that many products and services do "go together," usually because the same types of people tend to select them. In many cases, products do not seem to "make sense" if they are unaccompanied by companion products (for example, fast food and paper plates, or a suit and tie) or are incongruous in the presence of others (for example, a Chippendale chair in a high-tech office or Lucky Strike cigarettes with a solid gold lighter).

Therefore, an important part of lifestyle marketing is identifying the set of products and services that consumers seem to link together into a specific lifestyle. And research evidence suggests that even a relatively unattractive product becomes more appealing when consumers link it with other, liked products. Marketers who pursue co-branding strategies where they team up with other companies to promote their products understand this. For example, Wendy's and Procter & Gamble joined forces to offer Wendy's Custom Bean, a Folgers Gourmet Selection coffee that the restaurant chain says will become a centerpiece of its new breakfast menu. Some marketers even match up their spokescharacters in ads; the Pillsbury Doughboy appeared in a commercial with the Sprint Guy to pitch cellphones, the lonely Maytag repairman was in an ad for the Chevrolet Impala, and the Taco Bell Chihuahua showed up in a commercial for Geico insurance.

Product complementarity occurs when the symbolic meanings of different products relate to one another. Consumers use these sets of products we call a consumption constellation to define, communicate, and perform social roles. For example, we defined the American "yuppie" of the 1980s by such products as a Rolex watch, a BMW automobile, a Gucci briefcase, a squash racket, fresh pesto, white wine, and brie cheese. We find somewhat similar constellations for "Sloane Rangers" in the United Kingdom and "Bon Chic Bon Genres" in France. Although people today take pains to avoid being classified as yuppies, this social role had a major influence on defining cultural values and consumption priorities in the 1980s.

One powerful perspective that is based on understanding complex patterns of consumption is geodemography. This describes a set of analytical techniques that combine large amounts of data on consumer expenditures and other socioeconomic factors with geographic information about the areas in which people live, to identify consumers who share common consumption patterns. Researchers base this approach on the common assumption that "birds of a feather flock together." People who have similar needs and tastes also tend to live near one another. So, it should be possible to locate "pockets" of like-minded people who marketers can reach more economically by direct mail and other methods. A marketer who wants to reach white, single consumers who are college educated and tend to be fiscally conservative may find that it is more efficient to mail catalogs to zip codes 20770 (Greenbelt, Maryland) and 90277 (Redondo Beach, California) than to adjoining areas in either Maryland or California, where there are fewer consumers who exhibit these characteristics. Birds of a feather do buy together.

> People who have similar needs and tastes also tend to live near one another.

23

They think your product sucks—but that's not a bad thing

Have you checked out one of those crazy Mentos/Diet Coke videos yet? At least 800 of them flooded the Internet after people discovered that when you drop the quarter-size candies into bottles of Diet Coke, you get a geyser that shoots 20 feet into the air. Needless to say, Mentos got a gusher of free publicity out of the deal, too.

Consumer-generated content—where everyday people voice their opinions about products, brands, and companies on blogs, podcasts, and social networking sites like Facebook and MySpace, and even film their own commercials that thousands view on sites like YouTube—probably is the biggest marketing phenomenon of the past few years (even bigger than the iPhone or Paris Hilton's jail stay!). This important trend helps to define the era of so-called *Web 2.0*—the rebirth of the Internet as a social, interactive medium from its original roots as a form of one-way transmission from producers to consumers.

Although many marketers find this change threatening because they are now forced to "share" ownership of their brands with users, this new form of user participation is here to stay. The reality is that companies no longer can rely solely upon a "push method" to inform their customers about their products; there is now a vibrant two-way dialogue that allows consumers to contribute their evaluations of products within their respective Web communities.

Consumers are embracing this trend for several reasons: The technology is readily available and inexpensive to use; Internet access allows any surfer to become (somewhat of) an expert on anything in a matter of hours; and people trust their peers' opinions more than they do those of big companies. So, marketers need to accept this new reality—even when they don't necessarily like what customers have to say about their brands. When it comes to consumer-generated content, they're either on the train or under it! Here are a few of the many consumer-generated campaigns we've seen recently:

> Companies no longer can rely solely upon a "push method" to inform their customers about their products.

- At MasterCard's priceless.com Web site, consumers can write advertising copy for two filmed commercials by contributing four lines of dialogue, ending with the kicker, "Priceless."

- A Converse campaign that allowed customers to send in homemade commercials to Conversegallery.com attracted about 1,500 submissions. Converse ran several of them on television.

- Kao Corp., which makes Ban deodorant, asked young women to create ads that talk to fellow teens who worry about underarm odor. Readers of teen magazines submitted an image and filled in the blanks in the company's "Ban It" slogan. One typical submission shows four girls in similar jeans and tank tops, with their backs to the camera and the headline: "Ban Uniformity."

- PepsiCo sponsored a Creative Challenge in China that invited consumers to develop the next Pepsi TV commercial starring Asian pop-music superstar Jay Chou. Pepsi got almost 27,000 scripts in six weeks. To help promote the contest, China's Back Dorm Boys, a pair of lip-syncing "net celebrities" that Pepsi sponsored, acted out scripts in their dorm room. In the United States, Pepsi offered consumers a chance to design a new can for the beverage, with the winning design appearing on 500 million Pepsi cans.

- Lucasfilm made clips of Star Wars available to fans on the Internet to mash up (remix) at will to celebrate the 30th anniversary of the epic's release. Working with an easy-to-use editing program, fans can cut, add to, and retool the clips. Then they can post their creations to blogs or social networking sites like MySpace.

- Now that TV spin-offs from the Star Trek series have ended, bereft fans are filling the void by banding together to make their own episodes. Up to two dozen of these fan-made "Star Trek" projects are in various stages of completion, depending on what you count as a full-fledged production. You can view a Scottish production at www.ussintrepid.org.uk. A Los Angeles group has filmed more than 40 episodes, some of which explore gay themes that the original didn't get near. (Check out www. hiddenfrontier.com.)

- The Nokia Concept Lounge invited designers in Europe to share ideas for the next new, cool phone, while Nespresso's contest yielded coffee-drinking ideas like the Nespresso InCar coffee machine and the Nespresso Chipcard that, upon being inserted into a vending machine, communicates with a central database to brew a personalized cup of coffee.

Chevrolet learned the hard way about the downside of giving control over its brands to consumers. The carmaker introduced a Web site allowing visitors to take existing video clips and music, insert their own words, and create a customized 30-second commercial for the 2007 Chevrolet Tahoe. The idea was to generate interest for the Tahoe by encouraging satisfied drivers to circulate videos of themselves around the Web. Sure enough, plenty of videos circulated—but many of the messages for the gas-hungry SUV weren't exactly flattering. One ad used a sweeping view of the Tahoe being driven through a desert. "Our planet's oil is almost gone," it said. "You don't need G.P.S. to see where this road leads." Another commercial asked: "Like this snowy wilderness? Better get your fill of it now. Then say hello to global warming." A spokeswoman for Chevrolet commented, "We anticipated that there would be critical submissions. You do turn over your brand to the public, and we knew that we were going to get some bad with the good. But it's part of playing in this space."[46]

Indeed. If you're worried about what some of your customers might say about your brand, get over it. Listen to their complaints and improve your product rather than shutting the comments down.

> If you're worried about what some of your customers might say about your brand, get over it.

TRUTH

24

When to sell the steak, when to sell the sizzle

Should marketers worry more about what is said, or how it's said and who says it?

The answer is (drum roll)...it depends. Your target market's level of involvement with your product determines how much effort they will put into processing what you say. The situation is comparable to a traveler who comes to a fork in the road. She chooses one path or the other, and this choice has a big impact on the factors that will make a difference in persuasion attempts.

Depending on the personal relevance of this information, your customer will follow one of two routes to persuasion. Under conditions of high involvement, she takes the *central route*. Under conditions of low involvement, she takes a *peripheral route* instead. Let's take a closer look at each route:

> Your customer will follow one of two routes to persuasion.

The Central Route to Persuasion—
When the consumer finds the information in a persuasive message to be relevant or somehow interesting, she will carefully attend to the message content. In this case, she's likely to actively think about the arguments the marketer presents and generate *cognitive responses* to these arguments. On hearing a radio message warning about drinking while pregnant, an expectant mother might say to herself, "She's right. I really should stop drinking alcohol now that I'm pregnant." Or she might offer counterarguments, such as "That's a bunch of baloney. My mother had a cocktail every night when she was pregnant with me, and I turned out fine." If a person generates counterarguments in response to a message, it is less likely that she will yield to the message, whereas if she generates further supporting arguments, it's most likely she'll comply. The implication is that message factors, such as the quality of arguments an ad presents, will determine attitude change. Prior knowledge about a topic results in more thoughts about the message and increases the number of counterarguments. Sell the steak.

The Peripheral Route to Persuasion—We take the peripheral route when we're not motivated to think about the arguments that the marketer gives us. Instead, we're likely to use other cues to decide how to react to the message. These cues include the product's package, the attractiveness of the source, or the context in which the message appears. We call sources of information extraneous to the actual message *peripheral cues* because they surround the actual message.

When consumers don't care about a product, the style in which it's presented becomes more important.

The peripheral route to persuasion highlights an interesting paradox: When consumers don't care about a product, the style in which it's presented (for example, who endorses it or which visuals go with it) becomes more important. The implication here is that we may buy low-involvement products chiefly because the marketer has done a good job in designing a "sexy" package, choosing a popular spokesperson, or perhaps just creating a pleasant shopping environment. Sell the sizzle.

TRUTH

25

People are dumber than robots (lazier, too)

Consider the following scenario: You've scored a free ticket to a major football game. At the last minute, though, a sudden snowstorm makes getting to the stadium somewhat dangerous. Would you still go? Now, assume the same game and snowstorm, except this time you paid handsomely for the ticket. Would you head out in the storm in this case?

Analyses of people's responses to this situation and to other similar puzzles illustrate principles of *mental accounting*. This process demonstrates that the way we pose a problem (we call this *framing*) and whether it's phrased in terms of gains or losses influences our decisions.[47] In this case, researchers find that people are more likely to risk their personal safety in the storm if they paid for the football ticket than if it's a freebie. Only the most die-hard fan would fail to recognize that this is an irrational choice, as the risk is the same regardless of whether you got a great deal on the ticket. Researchers call this decision-making bias the *sunk-cost fallacy*—having paid for something makes us reluctant to waste it.

At the risk of understatement, many of the decisions customers make aren't rational—or even in their best interest. For example, the degree of external search we do for most products is surprisingly small, even when we would benefit by having more information. And lower-income shoppers, who have more to lose by making a bad purchase, actually search less prior to buying than do more affluent people.

Indeed, many consumers typically visit only one or two stores and rarely seek out unbiased information sources prior to making a purchase decision, especially when they have little time available to do so. This pattern is especially prevalent for decisions about durable goods such as appliances or autos, even when these products represent significant investments. One study of Australian car buyers found that more than a third had made two or fewer trips to inspect cars prior to buying one.[48]

Many of the decisions customers make aren't rational—or even in their best interest.

In addition, consumers can be amazingly fickle. They often engage in brand switching, even if their current brand satisfies their needs. For example, researchers for British brewer Bass Export who were studying the American beer market discovered a consumer trend toward having a repertoire of two to six favorite brands, rather than sticking to only one. This preference for brand switching led the firm to begin exporting its Tennent's 1885 lager to the United States, positioning the brew as an alternative to young drinkers' usual favorite brands. Sometimes, it seems that people just plain like to try new things—we crave variety as a form of stimulation or to reduce boredom. Variety seeking, the desire to choose new alternatives over more familiar ones, even influences us to switch from our favorite products to ones we like less! This can occur even before we become *satiated* or tired of our favorite. Research supports the idea that we are willing to trade enjoyment for variety simply because the unpredictability itself is rewarding.

Another irrational impulse we often experience is *loss aversion*. This means that we emphasize our losses more than our gains. For example, for most people, losing

> We emphasize our losses more than our gains.

money is more unpleasant than gaining money is pleasant. Our sense of risk differs when we face options involving gains versus those involving losses. To illustrate this bias, consider the following choices. For each, would you take the safe bet or choose to gamble?

> **Option 1**—You're given $30 and a chance to flip a coin: Heads you win $9; tails you lose $9.

> **Option 2**—Get $30 outright, or you accept a coin flip that will win you either $39 or $21.

In one study, 70 percent of those given option 1 chose to gamble, compared to just 43 percent of those offered option 2. Yet, the odds are the same for both options! The difference is that people prefer "playing with the house money"; they are more willing to take risks when they perceive they're using someone else's resources. So, contrary to a rational decision-making perspective, we value money differently depending on where it comes from. This explains, for example, why someone might choose to blow a big bonus on some frivolous purchase but would never consider taking that same amount out of her savings account for this purpose.

Finally, research in mental accounting demonstrates that extraneous characteristics of the choice situation can influence our selections, even though they wouldn't if we were totally rational decision makers. As one example, researchers gave survey participants one of two versions of this scenario:

You are lying on the beach on a hot day. All you have to drink is ice water. For the past hour, you have been thinking about how much you would enjoy a nice cold bottle of your favorite brand of beer. A companion gets up to go make a phone call and offers to bring back a beer from the only nearby place where beer is sold (either a fancy resort hotel or a small, run-down grocery store, depending on the version you're given). He says that the beer might be expensive and asks how much you are willing to pay for it. What price do you tell him?

Participants who read the fancy resort version offered a median price of $2.65, but those who got the grocery store version were only willing to pay $1.50. In both versions, the consumption act is the same, the beer is the same, and they don't consume any "atmosphere" because they drink the beer on the beach.[49] So much for rational decision making!

TRUTH

26

Your customers have your brand on the brain

Is there a "buy button" in your brain? Some corporations are teaming up with neuroscientists to find out. This work in *neuromarketing* uses functional magnetic resonance imaging (F.M.R.I.), a brain-scanning device that tracks blood flow as we perform mental tasks. In recent years, researchers have discovered that regions such as the amygdala, the hippocampus, and the hypothalamus are dynamic switchboards that blend memory, emotions, and biochemical triggers. These interconnected neurons shape the ways that fear, panic, exhilaration, and social pressure influence our choices.

Is there a "buy button" in your brain?

Scientists know that specific regions of the brain light up in these scans to show increased blood flow when a person recognizes a face, hears a song, makes a decision, or senses deception. Now they are trying to harness this technology to measure consumers' reactions to movie trailers, choices about automobiles, the appeal of a pretty face, and loyalty to specific brands. British researchers recorded brain activity as shoppers toured a virtual store. They claim to have identified the neural region that becomes active when a shopper decides which product to pluck from a supermarket shelf. DaimlerChrysler took brain scans of men as they looked at photos of cars and confirmed that sports cars activated their reward centers. The company's scientists found that the most popular vehicles—the Porsche- and Ferrari-style sports cars—triggered activity in a section of the brain called the *fusiform face area*, which governs facial recognition. Apparently, the cars reminded the men of faces with two lit eyes.

A study that took brain scans of people as they drank competing soft-drink brands illustrates how loyalty to a brand colors our reactions even at a basic, physiological level. When the researchers monitored brain scans of 67 people who did a blind taste test of Coca-Cola and Pepsi, each soft drink lit up the brain's reward system, and the participants were evenly split as to which drink they preferred—even though three out of four participants said they preferred Coke. When told they were drinking Coke, the regions of the brain that control memory lit up, and this activation drowned out the area that reacts simply to taste cues. In this case, Coke's strong brand identity trumped the sensations coming from respondents' taste receptors.

DaimlerChrysler took brain scans of men as they looked at photos of cars and confirmed that sports cars activated their reward centers.

In another study, researchers reported that pictures of celebrities triggered many of the same brain circuits as images of shoes, cars, chairs, wristwatches, sunglasses, handbags, and water bottles. All of these objects set off a rush of activity in a part of the cortex that neuroscientists know links to a sense of identity and social image. The scientists also identified types of consumers based on their responses. At one extreme were people whose brains responded intensely to "cool" products and celebrities with bursts of activity but who didn't respond at all to "uncool" images. They dubbed these participants "cool fools," likely to be impulsive or compulsive shoppers. At the other extreme were people whose brains reacted only to the unstylish items, a pattern that fits well with people who tend to be anxious, apprehensive, or neurotic.

Many researchers remain skeptical about how helpful this technology will be for consumer research. If indeed researchers can reliably track consumers' brand preferences by seeing how their brains react, there may be many interesting potential opportunities for new research techniques that rely on what we (at least our brains) do rather than on what we say.

TRUTH

27

Let their mouseclicks do the walking

As anyone who's ever typed a search phrase like "home theatres" into Google knows, the Web delivers enormous amounts of product and retailer information in seconds. In fact, the biggest problem Web surfers face these days is narrowing down their choices, not beefing them up. In cyberspace, simplicity is The Holy Grail.

With the tremendous number of Web sites available and the huge number of people surfing the Web each day, how can people organize information and decide where to click? A cybermediary often is the answer. This is an intermediary that helps to filter and organize online market information so that customers can identify and evaluate alternatives more efficiently. Many consumers regularly link to comparison-shopping sites like Bizrate.com or Pricegrabbers.com, for example, to get a list of the online retailers that sell a given item along with the price each charges.

> The biggest problem Web surfers face these days is narrowing down their choices, not beefing them up.

Cybermediaries take different forms:

- Directories and portals like Yahoo! or The Knot are general services that tie together a large variety of different sites.

- Web site evaluators reduce the risk to consumers by reviewing sites and recommending the best ones. For example, Point Communications selects sites that it designates as Top 5 percent of the Web.

- Forums, fan clubs, and user groups offer product-related discussions to help customers sift through options. It's becoming clear that customer product reviews are a key driver of satisfaction and loyalty. In one large survey, about half of respondents who bought an item from a major Web site remembered seeing customer product reviews. This group's satisfaction with the online shopping experience was 5 percent higher than for shoppers who didn't recall customer reviews.[50] Another advantage is that consumers get to experience much wider options—and products like movies, books, and CDs that aren't "blockbusters" are more likely to sell. At NetFlix, the online DVD rental company, for example, fellow subscribers recommend about two-thirds of the films that people order. In fact, between 70 and 80 percent of NetFlix rentals come from the company's back catalog of 38,000 films rather than recent releases.

Incidentally, this aspect of online customer review is one important factor that's fueling a new way of thinking that writer Chris Anderson calls the long tail. The basic idea is that we need no longer rely solely on big hits (like blockbuster movies or best-selling books) to find profits. Companies can also make money by selling small numbers of items that only a few people want—if they sell enough different items. For example, Amazon. com maintains an inventory of 3.7 million books compared to the 100,000 or so you'll find in a Barnes & Noble retail store. Most of these will sell only a few thousand copies (if that), but the 3.6 million books that Barnes & Noble doesn't carry make up a quarter of Amazon's revenues! Other examples of the long tail include successful microbreweries and TV networks that make money on reruns of old shows on channels like the Game Show Network.

■ Financial intermediaries authorize payments from buyer to seller. Payment systems include electronic equivalents to credit card charges (PayPal), writing checks (Checkfree), paying in cash (Digicash), and sending secure electronic mail authorizing a payment (First Virtual).

■ Intelligent agents are sophisticated software programs that use collaborative filtering technologies to learn from past user behavior to recommend new purchases. For example, when you let Amazon.com suggest a new book, it's using an intelligent agent to propose novels based on what you and others like you have bought in the past. Collaborative filtering is still in its infancy. In the next few years, expect to see many new Web-based methods to simplify the consumer decision-making process. Now if only someone could come up with an easier way to pay for all the great stuff you find courtesy of shopping bots!

Researchers are working hard to understand how consumers go about finding information online and, in particular, how they react to and integrate recommendations they receive from different kinds of online agents into their own product choices. An electronic recommendation agent is a software tool that tries to understand the criteria a human decision maker uses to choose among competitors within a product category via a series of questions about what the person likes and dislikes. Based on that data, the software then recommends a list of alternatives sorted by the degree that they fit these criteria. The Music Genome Project is one of the newest technologies that enable music fans to discover new artists. At Pandora.com, you type in the name of a band or song and immediately begin hearing similar tunes that the site's recommender system has determined you'll enjoy. By rating songs and artists, you can refine the suggestions, allowing Pandora to create a truly personalized station. The service employs 45 analysts, many with music degrees, who rank 15,000 songs a month on 400 characteristics. Similarly, Liveplasma.com graphically "maps" consumers' interests in movies and music. If you search for music by The Decemberists, for example, you'll get a graphical representation of what previous Decemberists customers have purchased, presented in clusters of circles of various sizes. The bigger the circle, the greater the popularity of that band.

Research on how consumers use intelligent agents is starting to connect the dots regarding just how influential these digital decision aids are.

- Consumers who consult recommendation agents select the recommended products twice as often as those who do not.

- The extent to which a consumer has agreed with the agent on past recommendations influences the likelihood he will accept the advice now.

- Recommendation agents have a greater impact on decisions when consumers feel the decision is risky—for example, if the consequences of making a poor decision are high or if the item is expensive.

- When a recommendation agent asks the consumer about his preferences for a particular product attribute, the consumer will weigh that attribute more when making an actual product choice.

Consumers who consult recommendation agents select the recommended products twice as often as those who do not.

28

Nothing shouts quality like leather from Poland

A product's "address" matters. We seek out Italian shoes and microwave ovens built in South Korea, but we may take a pass on Italian ovens and South Korean shoes. Consumers strongly associate certain items with specific countries, and products from those countries often attempt to benefit from these linkages. In addition, the consumer's own expertise with the product category moderates the effects of this attribute. When other information is available, experts tend to ignore country-of-origin information, whereas novices continue to rely on it. However, when other information is unavailable or ambiguous, both experts and novices will rely on a product's birthplace to make a decision.

Predicting the quality of a product by looking at its country of origin is but one example of a common strategy that customers use all the time. Instead of thinking carefully about the pros and cons of a purchase, we often rely on heuristics—mental rules-of-thumb that lead to a speedy decision. These rules range from the very general ("higher-priced products are higher-quality products" or "buy the same brand I bought last time") to the very specific ("buy Domino, the brand of sugar my mother always bought" or "you can't go wrong with shoes from Italy").

One shortcut we often use is to infer hidden dimensions of products from attributes we can observe. In these cases, the visible element acts as a product signal that communicates some underlying quality. This explains why someone trying to sell a used car makes sure the car's exterior is clean and shiny: Potential buyers often judge the vehicle's mechanical condition by its appearance, even though this means they may drive away in a clean, shiny clunker.

> Instead of thinking carefully about the pros and cons of a purchase, we often rely on *heuristics*—mental rules-of-thumb that lead to a speedy decision.

When we have only incomplete product information, we often base our judgments on our beliefs about *covariation*—the associations we have among events that may or may not actually influence one another. For example, a shopper may judge product quality by the length of time a manufacturer has been in business. Other signals or attributes that consumers tend to believe coexist with good or bad products include well-known brand names, country of origin, price, and the retail outlets that carry the product.

Unfortunately, many of us estimate covariation quite poorly. And our erroneous beliefs persist despite evidence to the contrary—we tend to see what we're looking for. In other words, we look for product information that confirms our guesses and ignore or explain away information that contradicts what we already think. In one experiment, consumers sampled four sets of products to determine their price related to their quality. Those who believed prior to the study that a higher price means higher quality elected to sample higher-priced products, thus creating a self-fulfilling prophecy.[51]

How valid are heuristics? For example, do higher prices in fact mean higher quality? This *price—quality relationship* is one of the most pervasive heuristics around. Novice consumers may, in fact, consider price as the only relevant product attribute. Experts also consider this information, although they tend to use price for its informational value, especially for products (for example, virgin wool) that they know vary widely in quality. When this quality level is

> We look for product information that confirms our guesses and ignore or explain away information that contradicts what we already think.

more standard or strictly regulated (for example, Harris Tweed sport coats), experts do not weigh price in their decisions. For the most part, this belief is justified; you do tend to get what you pay for. However, let the buyer beware: The price-quality relationship is not always justified.

TRUTH
29

Consider investing in a drive-thru mortuary

It's no secret that environmental factors influence what we feel like buying, not to mention how much. One study even reported that pumping certain odors into a Las Vegas casino actually increased the amount of money patrons fed into slot machines!

A particularly important situational factor is simply how pressed we are for time—and we often feel we are. Many consumers believe they are more pressed for time than ever before—a feeling marketers call time poverty. This feeling appears to be due more to perception than to fact. The reality is that we just have more options for spending our time, so we feel pressured by the weight of all these choices. The average working day at the turn of the twentieth century was 10 hours (six days per week), and women did 27 hours of housework per week, compared to less than five hours weekly now. About a third of Americans report always feeling rushed—up from 25 percent of the population in 1964.[52]

> Many consumers believe they are more pressed for time than ever before—a feeling marketers call *time poverty*.

Our experience of time is largely a result of our culture, because different societies have varying perspectives on this experience. To most Western consumers, time is a neatly compartmentalized thing: We wake up in the morning, go to school or work, come home, eat dinner, go out, go to sleep, wake up, and do it all over again. We call this perspective *linear separable time*: Events proceed in an orderly sequence, and "There's a time and a place for everything." There is a clear sense of past, present, and future. We perform many activities as the means to some end that will occur later, as when we "save for a rainy day."

This perspective seems "natural" to us, but not all others share it. Some cultures run on *procedural time* and ignore the clock completely—people simply decide to do something "when the time is right." For example, in Burundi people might arrange to meet when the cows return from the watering hole. If you ask someone in Madagascar how long it takes to get to the market, you will get an answer like, "in the time it takes to cook rice."

Alternatively, in circular or cyclic time, natural cycles, such as the regular occurrence of the seasons, govern people's sense of time (a perspective many Hispanic cultures share). To these consumers, the notion of the future does not make sense—that time will be much like the present. Because the concept of future value does not exist, these consumers often prefer to buy an inferior product that is available now rather than wait for a better one that may be available later. Also, it is hard to convince people who function on circular time to buy insurance or save for a rainy day when they don't think in terms of a linear future.

The psychological dimension of time—how we actually experience it—is an important factor in queuing theory, the mathematical study of waiting lines. As we all know, our experience while waiting for something has a big effect on our evaluations of what we get at the end of the wait. Although we assume that something must be pretty good if we have to wait for it, the negative feelings that long waits arouse can quickly turn people off. In a recent survey, NCR Corp. found that standing around the local Department or Division of Motor Vehicles is the most dreaded wait of all. Waiting in line at retail outlets came in a close second, followed by registering at clinics or hospitals, checking in at airports, and ordering at fast-food restaurants or deli counters. On average, consumers estimate that they spend more than two days per year waiting in line for service, and half believe they waste between 30 minutes to two hours each week waiting for service.[53]

> Our experience while waiting for something has a big effect on our evaluations of what we get at the end of the wait.

Marketers use "tricks" to minimize psychological waiting time (just think about your last visit to Disney World). These techniques range from altering customers' perceptions of a line's length to providing distractions that divert attention away from waiting. One hotel chain, after receiving excessive complaints about the wait for elevators, installed mirrors near the elevator banks. People's natural tendency to check their appearance reduced complaints, even though the actual waiting time was unchanged.

TRUTH

30

Go to the Gemba

How much are your favorite pants worth? A judge in Washington, D.C. made headlines when he filed a $54 million lawsuit against his neighborhood dry cleaner that he accused of losing a pair of his pinstriped suit pants. He claimed that a D.C. consumer protection law entitled him to thousands of dollars for each day over nearly four years in which signs at the shop promised "same day service" and "satisfaction guaranteed." The suit dragged on for several months, but at the end of the day, the plaintiff went home with empty pockets.

If you're not happy with a product or service, what can you do about it? You have three possible courses of action (though sometimes you can take more than one).

- **Voice response**—You can appeal directly to the retailer for redress (for example, a refund).

- **Private response**—You can express your dissatisfaction to friends and boycott the product or the store where you bought it.

- **Third-party response**—Like the pantsless judge, you can take legal action against the merchant, register a complaint with the Better Business Bureau, or perhaps write a letter to the newspaper.

In one study, business majors wrote complaint letters to companies. When the company sent a free sample in response, this significantly improved their feelings about the company. This didn't happen, however, when they received only a letter of apology but no swag. Even worse, students who got no response reported an even more negative image than before, indicating that *any* kind of response is better than none.[54]

A number of factors influence which route to dealing with dissatisfaction we will choose. People are more likely to take action for expensive products such as household durables, cars, and clothing than for inexpensive products. Ironically, consumers who are satisfied with a store in general are more likely to complain if they experience something bad; they take the time to complain because they feel connected to the store. Older people are also more likely to complain, and they are much more likely to believe the store will actually resolve the problem. Shoppers who get their problems resolved feel even *better* about the store than if nothing had gone wrong. However, if the consumer does not believe that the store will respond well to a complaint, the person will be more likely to simply switch than fight. The moral: Marketers should *encourage* consumers to complain to them.

Shoppers who get their problems resolved feel even better about the store than if nothing had gone wrong.

People are more likely to spread the word about unresolved negative experiences to their friends than they are to boast about positive occurrences.

To be more responsive to its customers, Dell created a social networking community it calls *Idea Storm*. This is an online forum for users to submit suggestions about its products, and people have deluged the site with thousands of recommendations and comments. Increasingly, companies are figuring out that they're better off revealing their flaws to their customers than pretending to be foolproof—and having to explain away failures later. For example, Delta Airlines (an established player in an industry notorious for low customer satisfaction) recently created its own Web site, http://blog. delta.com, that hosts suggestions from consumers—"Bring the pillows back, please"—as well as polls about features and offerings.

Many analysts who study consumer satisfaction or who are trying to design new products or services to increase it recognize that it is crucial to understand how people actually interact with their environment to identify potential problems. They typically conduct these investigations in focus groups where a small set of consumers comes into a facility to try a new item while company personnel observe them from behind a mirror.

However, some researchers advocate a more up-close-and-personal approach that allows them to watch people in the actual environment where they consume the product. This perspective grew out of the Japanese approach to *total quality management* (*TQM*); a complex set of management and engineering procedures aimed at reducing errors and increasing quality.

> It's essential to send marketers and designers to the precise place where consumers *use* the product or service rather than asking laboratory subjects to interact with it in a simulated environment.

To help them achieve more insight, these researchers go to the *Gemba*, which to the Japanese means the one true source of information. According to this philosophy, it's essential to send marketers and designers to the precise place where consumers *use* the product or service rather than asking laboratory subjects to interact with it in a simulated environment.

Host Foods, which operates food concessions in major airports, sent a team to the *Gemba*—in this case, an airport cafeteria—to identify problem areas. Employees watched as customers chose to (or didn't) enter the facility and then followed them as they inspected the menu, procured silverware, paid, and found a table. The findings were crucial to Host's redesign of the facility to make it easier to use. For example, the team identified a common problem that many people traveling solo experience: the need to put down one's luggage to enter the food line, and the feeling of panic you get because you're not able to keep an eye on your valuables while you're getting your meal.

Get out of your office, and experience your product or service precisely the way your customers do. You may be in for a rude awakening.

TRUTH

31

Your customers want to be like Mike (or someone like him)

Will a few pieces of leather and rubber really improve your game? In the movie *Like Mike*, the main character believes that he can fly higher when he dons his magical Air Jordans. Even those of us who would need a rocket pack to jump higher still get caught up in beliefs like this—if we didn't, all those sweet celebrity endorsement deals would be "nothing but net." Whether we're influenced by another individual or by a group, many of our product choices are strongly influenced by what others do. (No, this force didn't go away after junior high school.) A *reference group* is "an actual or imaginary individual or group that significantly influences the way we think about ourselves and the things we buy. It's hard to discount the power these groups exert upon us.

For example, in the United States and around the world, many thousands of weekend Hell's Angels drop huge sums on motorcycles and biker paraphernalia. Harley-Davidson's most important marketing tool is not slick TV ads but its network of Harley Owners Groups (HOGs) that provide a feeling of community and camaraderie to members. Fellow riders bond via their consumption choices, so total strangers feel an immediate connection with one another when they meet. The publisher of *American Iron*, an industry magazine, observed, "You don't buy a Harley because it's a superior bike; you buy a Harley to be a part of a family."[55]

> Many of our product choices are strongly influenced by what others do.

Why are reference groups so persuasive? The answer lies in the social power they wield over us. You have power over another person if you can make him do something—even if that person does it willingly. Social scientists describe several categories of social power.

- **Referent power**—If a person admires the qualities of a person or a group, he tries to imitate them by copying the referent's behaviors (for example, choice of clothing, cars, and leisure activities). Prominent people in all walks of life can affect our consumption behaviors by virtue of product endorsements (50 Cent for Reebok), distinctive fashion statements (Fergie's displays of high-end designer clothing), or championing causes (Lance Armstrong's work for cancer). Referent power is important to many marketing strategies because consumers voluntarily modify what they do and buy to identify with a referent.

> You have power over another person if you can make him do something—even if that person does it willingly.

■ **Information power**—A person can have power simply because she knows something others would like to know. Editors of trade publications such as Women's Wear Daily often possess tremendous power because of their ability to compile and disseminate information that can make or break individual designers or companies.

■ **Legitimate power**—Sometimes we grant power by virtue of social agreements, such as the authority we give to police officers, soldiers, and yes, sometimes even professors. The legitimate power that a uniform confers wields authority in consumer contexts, including teaching hospitals where medical students don white coats to enhance their standing with patients. Marketers may "borrow" this form of power to influence consumers. For example, an ad featuring a model wearing a white doctor's coat can add an aura of legitimacy or authority to the presentation of the product. ("I'm not a doctor, but I play one on TV.")

■ **Expert power**—To attract the casual Internet user, U.S. Robotics signed up British physicist Stephen Hawking to endorse its modems. A company executive commented, "We wanted to generate trust. So we found visionaries who use U.S. Robotics technology, and we let them tell the consumer how it makes their lives more productive." Hawking, who has Lou Gehrig's disease and speaks via a synthesizer, said in one TV spot, "My body may be stuck in this chair, but with the Internet, my mind can go to the end of the universe." Hawking's expert power derives from the knowledge he possesses about a content area. This helps to explain the weight many of us assign to professional critics' reviews of restaurants, books, movies, and cars—even though, with the advent of blogs and open-source references such as Wikipedia, it's getting a lot harder to tell just who is really an expert!

■ **Reward power**—A person or group with the means to provide positive reinforcement has reward power. The reward may be the tangible kind, such as what the contestants on *Survivor* experience when they get to stay on the island. Or it can be more intangible, such as the approval that the judges on *American Idol* (except Simon) deliver to contestants.

■ **Coercive power**—We exert coercive power when we influence someone because of social or physical intimidation. A threat is often effective in the short term, but it doesn't tend to stick because we usually revert back to our original behavior as soon as the bully leaves the scene. Fortunately, marketers rarely try to use this type of power—unless you count those annoying calls from telemarketers! However, we can see elements of this power base in fear appeals that some companies use to scare us into buying life insurance ("who knows when you might walk into a bus?") as well as in intimidating salespeople who try to succeed with a "hard sell."

TRUTH

32

Go tribal

Before it released the popular Xbox game Halo 2, Microsoft put up a Web site to explain the story line. However, there was a catch: The story was written from the point of view of the Covenant (the aliens who are preparing to attack Earth in the game)—and in their language. Within 48 hours, avid gamers around the world worked together by sharing information in gaming chat rooms to crack the code and translate the text. More than 1.5 million people preordered the game before its release. This cooperative effort illustrates a major trend in consumer behavior.

A *brand community* is a group of consumers who share a set of social relationships based on usage or interest in a product. Unlike other kinds of communities, these members typically don't live near each other—except when they may meet for brief periods at organized events or *brandfests* that community-oriented companies such as Jeep, Saturn, or Harley-Davidson sponsor. These events help owners to "bond" with fellow enthusiasts and strengthen their identification with the product as well as with others they meet who share their passion. Researchers find that people who participate in these events feel more positive about the products as a result, and this enhances brand loyalty. They are more forgiving than others of product failures or lapses in service quality, and they're less likely to switch brands even if they learn that competing products are as good or better. Furthermore, these community members become emotionally involved in the company's welfare, and they often serve as brand missionaries by carrying its marketing message to others.

> A *brand community* is a group of consumers who share a set of social relationships based on usage or interest in a product.

A *consumer tribe* is similar to a brand community; it is a group of people who share a lifestyle and who can identify with each other because of a shared allegiance to an activity or a product. Although these tribes are often unstable and short-lived, at least for a time members identify with others through shared emotions, moral beliefs, styles of life, and, of course, the products they jointly consume as part of their tribal affiliation. Some companies, especially those that are more youth-oriented, rely on a *tribal marketing strategy* that links their product to, say, a group of shredders (skateboarders to us ancient folks). However, there also are plenty of tribes with older members, such as car enthusiasts who gather to celebrate such cult products as the Citroën in Europe and the Ford Mustang in the United States, or "foodies" who share their passion for cooking with

Community members become emotionally involved in the company's welfare, and they often serve as brand missionaries by carrying its marketing message to others.

other Wolfgang Puck wannabees around the world. Pontiac opened a community hub on Yahoo! it calls Pontiac Underground—"Where Passion for Pontiac Is Driven By You." The carmaker does no overt marketing on the site; the idea is to let drivers find it and spread the word themselves. Users share photos and videos of cars using Flickr and Yahoo! Video. A Yahoo! Answers zone enables knowledge sharing. Meanwhile, a list of Pontiac clubs in the physical world and on Yahoo! Groups allows users to connect offline and online.

TRUTH

33

People like to do their own thing—so long as it's everyone else's thing too

The early Bohemians who lived in Paris around 1830 made a point of behaving, well, differently from others. One flamboyant figure of the time became famous for walking a lobster on a leash through the gardens of the Royal Palace. His friends drank wine from human skulls, cut their beards in strange shapes, and slept in tents on the floors of their garrets. Sounds a bit like some fraternity houses we've visited.

Although in every age there certainly are those who "march to their own drummers," most people tend to follow society's expectations regarding how they should act and look (with a little improvisation here and there, of course). *Conformity* is a change in beliefs or actions as a reaction to real or imagined group pressure. For a society to function, its members develop norms, or informal rules that govern behavior. Without these rules, we would have chaos. Imagine the confusion if a simple norm such as stopping for a red traffic light did not exist.

We conform in many small ways every day—even though we don't always realize it. Unspoken rules govern many aspects of consumption. In addition to norms regarding appropriate use of clothing and other personal items, we conform to rules that include gift-giving (we expect birthday presents from loved ones and get upset if they do not materialize), sex roles (men often pick up the check on a first date), and personal hygiene (our friends expect us to shower regularly).

We don't mimic others' behavior all the time, so what makes it more likely we'll conform? These are some common culprits:

■ **Cultural pressures**—Different cultures encourage conformity to a greater or lesser degree. The American slogan "Do your own thing" in the 1960s reflected a movement away from conformity and toward individualism. In contrast, Japanese society emphasizes collective well-being and group loyalty over individuals' needs.

> We conform in many small ways every day—even though we don't always realize it.

■ **Fear of deviance**—The individual may have reason to believe that the group will apply *sanctions* to punish nonconforming behaviors. It's not unusual to observe adolescents shunning a peer who is "different" or a corporation or university passing over a person for promotion because she is not a "team player."

■ **Commitment**—The more people who are dedicated to a group and value their membership in it, the more motivated they are to do what the group wants. Rock groupies and followers of TV evangelists may do anything their idols ask of them, and terrorists are willing to die for their cause. According to the *principle of least interest*, the person who is *least* committed to staying in a relationship has the most power, because that party doesn't care as much if the other person rejects him.

■ **Group unanimity, size, and expertise**—As groups gain in power, compliance increases. It is often harder to resist the demands of a large number of people than only a few—especially when a "mob mentality" rules.

■ **Susceptibility to interpersonal influence**—This personality trait refers to an individual's need to have others think highly of him. Consumers who don't possess this trait are *role-relaxed*; they tend to be older, affluent, and highly confident. Subaru created a communications strategy to reach role-relaxed consumers. In one of its commercials, a man proclaims, "I want a car....Don't tell me about wood paneling, about winning the respect of my neighbors. They're my neighbors. They're not my heroes."

Intrepid marketers don't fear: These consumers are in the minority. Most of us are mindful of what our friends and neighbors buy, and people who belong to groups do tend to display patterns of similarity—even *after* high school!

> The more people who are dedicated to a group and value their membership in it, the more motivated they are to do what the group wants.

TRUTH

34

Catch a buzz

Altoids breath mints had been around for 200 years, but suddenly their popularity skyrocketed. How did this happen? The revival began when the mint began to attract a devoted following among smokers and coffee drinkers who hung out in the blossoming Seattle club scene during the 1980s. Until 1993, when Kraft bought manufacturer Callard & Bowers, only those "in the know" sucked the mints. The brand's marketing manager persuaded Kraft to hire advertising agency Leo Burnett to develop a modest promotional campaign. The agency decided to publicize the candy with subway posters sporting retro imagery and other "low-tech" media to avoid making the product seem mainstream—that would turn off the original audience. As young people started to tune into this "retro" treat, its popularity rocketed.

As the Altoids success story illustrates, "buzz" makes a hit product. *Word of mouth (WOM)* is product information that individuals transmit to other individuals. Because we get the word from people we know, WOM tends to be more reliable and trustworthy than messages from more formal marketing channels. And, unlike advertising, WOM often comes with social pressure to conform to these recommendations. Ironically, despite all the money that marketers pump into lavish ads, WOM is far more powerful: It influences two-thirds of all consumer goods sales.

So, how can marketers harness the enormous power of WOM? In the "old days" (a few years ago), a toy company would launch a new product by unveiling it during a Spring trade fair, and then it would run a November–December saturation television ad campaign during cartoon prime time to sell the toy to kids. In contrast, consider the Picoo Z helicopter, a $30 toy helicopter made by Silverlit Toys in Hong Kong. In March 2007, a Google search for the Picoo produced more than 109,000 URLs, whereas the URLs for Silverlit Toys was more than 597,000, with many of those links pointing to major online global gift retailers, such as Hammacher-Schlemmer and Toys-R-Us.

> WOM influences two-thirds of all consumer goods sales.

Do you think this huge exposure was the result of a meticulously planned promotional strategy? Think again. By most accounts, a 28-year-old tech worker in Chicago started the Picoo Z buzz when he bought his helicopter after reading about it on a hobbyist message board. A few months later, he uploaded his homemade video of the toy on YouTube. Within two weeks, 15 of his friends bought the toy, and they, in turn, posted their own videos and pointed viewers to the original video. Internet retailers who troll online conversations for fresh and exciting buzz identified the toy and started adding their own links to the clips. In just a few short months, there were hundreds of Picoo Z videos, and more than a million people viewed them.

So, how can you stimulate word of mouth? Consider enlisting brand ambassadors to announce a new brand or service. AT&T sent its ambassadors to high-traffic areas of California and New Jersey, doing random favors such as handing dog biscuits to people walking their dogs and providing binoculars to concertgoers to promote its new AT&T Local Service. Hyatt Hotels unleashed 100 bellhops in Manhattan, who spent the day opening doors, carrying packages, and handing out pillow mints to thousands of consumers.

Or go for *viral* marketing, the strategy of getting visitors to a Web site to forward information on the site to their friends to make still more consumers aware of the product—usually by creating online content that is entertaining or just plain weird. To promote a use for a razor that it could never discuss on TV, Philips launched a Norelco Web site, shaveeverywhere.com. The ad features a guy in a bathrobe explaining how to use the shaver

> Consider enlisting brand ambassadors to announce a new brand or service.

in places, well, not on your head. The site uses pictures of fruit and vegetables to refer to male body parts. This viral strategy did its job, as thousands of people worldwide forwarded the URL to their friends. Catch the buzz.

TRUTH
35

Go with the flow—
get shopmobbed today

Odds are you (or your kid) have already logged some serious time on Facebook, MySpace, or LinkedIn before you started reading this paragraph today. *Social networking*, where members post information about themselves and make contact with others who share similar interests and opinions, may well be the biggest development in consumer behavior since the TV dinner! Almost daily we hear about yet another social networking site where users can set up a home page with photos, a profile, and links to others in their social networks. They can browse for friends, dates, partners for activities, or contacts of all kinds and invite them to join the users' personal networks as "friends."

Social networking is an integral part of what many call Web 2.0, which is like the Internet on steroids. (Learn more about social networking in *The Truth About Profiting from Social Networking*.) The key change is the interactivity among producers and users, but these are some other characteristics of a *Web 2.0* site.

- It improves as the number of users increases. For example, Amazon's capability to recommend books to you based on what other people with similar interests have bought gets better as it tracks more and more people who are entering search queries.

- Its currency is eyeballs. Google makes its money by charging advertisers according to the number of people who see their ads after typing in a search term.

> Social networking is an integral part of what many call Web 2.0, which is like the Internet on steroids.

- It's version-free and in perpetual beta. *Wikipedia*, the online encyclopedia, gets updated constantly by users who "correct" others' errors.

- It categorizes entries according to "folksonomy" rather than "taxonomy." In other words, sites rely on users rather than preestablished systems to sort contents. Listeners at Pandora.com create their own "radio stations" that play songs by artists they choose, as well as other similar artists.

This last point highlights a key change in the way some new media companies approach their businesses: Think of it as marketing strategy by committee. The *wisdom of crowds* perspective (from a book by that name) argues that, under the right circumstances, groups are smarter than the smartest people in them. If this is true, it implies that large numbers of (nonexpert) consumers can predict successful products.

For example, at Threadless.com, customers rank T-shirt designs ahead of time, and the company prints the winning ideas. Every week, contestants upload T-shirts designs to the site, where about 700 compete to be among the six that it will print during that time. Threadless visitors score designs on a scale of 0 to 5, and the staff selects winners from the most popular entrants. The six lucky artists each get $2,000 in cash and merchandise. Threadless sells out of every shirt it offers.

> The *wisdom of crowds* perspective argues that, under the right circumstances, groups are smarter than the smartest people in them.

Here are some more crowd-based sites to watch:

- Sermo.com is a social network for physicians. It has no advertising, job listings, or membership fees. It makes its money (about $500,000 a year so far) by charging institutional investors for the opportunity to listen in as approximately 15,000 doctors chat among themselves. Say, for example, a young patient breaks out in hives after taking a new prescription. A doctor might post whether she thinks this is because of a rare symptom or perhaps the drug's side-effect. If other doctors feel it's the latter, this negative news could affect the drug manufacturer's stock, so their opinions have value to analysts. Doctors who ask or answer a question that paying observers deem especially valuable receive bonuses of $5 to $25 per post.

- How about social networking sites that "create" a concert by persuading an artist to perform in a certain city or country? At Eventful.com, fans can demand events and performances in their town and spread the word to make them happen. Or how about actually buying a piece of the bands you like? Go to SellaBand. com, where fans ("believers") buy "parts" in a band for $10 per share. After the band sells 5,000 parts, SellaBand arranges a professional recording, including top studios, A&R (Artists & Repertoire managers (industry talent scouts), and producers. Believers receive a limited edition CD of the recording. They also get a piece of the profits, so they're likely to promote the band wherever they can.

■ Individual consumers gain crowd clout by *shopmobbing* with strangers. So far, this is most popular in China, where the *tuangou* ("team purchase") phenomenon involves strangers organizing themselves around a specific product or service. Members who meet online at sites such as Taobao.com and Liba.com/index arrange to meet at a certain date and time in a real-world store and literally mob the unsuspecting retailer—the bargain-hungry crowd negotiates a group discount on the spot.

TRUTH

36

Find the market maven, and the rest is gravy

As Cold Stone Creamery expands to Japan, the ice cream store projects a somewhat different image than it has in the United States. The chain wants to be ultra cool by generating a buzz among fashion-conscious "office ladies," as the Japanese call young, single, female professionals. These women are very influential in Japan; their reactions to a new product can make or break it. To woo this group, Cold Stone sponsored a fashion show for young women (assuming the models can fit into the dresses after sampling a few of the chain's caloric creations), and fashion magazines staged photo shoots at the stores.

Although consumers get information from personal sources, they do not usually ask just *anyone* for advice about purchases. If you decide to buy a new stereo, you will most likely seek advice from a friend who knows a lot about sound systems. This friend may own a sophisticated system or may subscribe to specialized magazines such as *Stereo Review* and spend free time browsing through electronics stores. However, you may have another friend who has a reputation for being stylish and who spends his free time reading *Gentleman's Quarterly* and shopping at trendy boutiques. You might not bring up your stereo problem with him, but you may take him with you to shop for a new fall wardrobe.

Everyone knows people who are knowledgeable about products and whose advice others take seriously. Like one of the Japanese office ladies, this individual is an *opinion leader;* a person who is frequently able to influence others' attitudes or behavior. Clearly, some people's recommendations carry more weight than others. Opinion leaders are extremely valuable information sources because they prescreen, evaluate, and synthesize product information in an unbiased way. They tend to be socially active and highly interconnected in their communities. These individuals are often among the first to buy new products, so they absorb much of the risk. This experience reduces uncertainty for others who are not as courageous.

Some people's recommendations carry more weight than others.

Early conceptions of the opinion leader role assumed that the opinion leader absorbs information from the mass media and, in turn, transmits data to opinion receivers. This view has turned out to be overly simplified; it confuses the functions of several different types of consumers. Indeed, we now know that opinion leaders also are likely to be *opinion seekers*. They are generally more involved in a product category and actively search for information. As a result, they are more likely to talk about products with others and to solicit others' opinions. Contrary to the static view of opinion leadership, most product-related conversation does not take place in a "lecture" format in which one person does all the talking. (Even husbands get a word in now and then.) A lot of product-related conversation occurs in the context of a casual interaction rather than as formal instruction. One study, which found that opinion seeking is especially high for food products, revealed that two-thirds of opinion seekers also view themselves as opinion leaders.[56]

Consumers who are expert in a product category may not necessarily share their trade secrets with others but, on the other hand, we all know people who love to talk about what they buy— whether or not we want to hear about it. A *market maven* loves to transmit marketplace information of all types. These shopaholics are not necessarily interested in certain products, and they may not necessarily be early purchasers; they're simply into staying on top of what's happening in the marketplace. Researchers use the following scale items, to which respondents indicate how much they agree or disagree, to identify market mavens:[57]

1. I like introducing new brands and products to my friends.
2. I like helping people by providing them with information about many kinds of products.
3. People ask me for information about products, places to shop, or sales.
4. If someone asked me where to get the best buy on several types of products, I could tell him or her where to shop.
5. My friends think of me as a good source of information when it comes to new products or sales.

Ironically, marketers often overlook yet another type of consumer in their quest to convince shoppers to buy. A *surrogate consumer* is a person whom we hire to provide input into our purchase decisions. Unlike the opinion leader or market maven, the surrogate is usually compensated for his advice. Interior decorators, stockbrokers, professional shoppers, and college consultants are surrogate consumers.

Regardless of whether they actually make the purchase on behalf of the consumer, surrogates' recommendations can be enormously influential. The consumer, in essence, relinquishes control over several or all decision-making functions, such as information search, evaluation of alternatives, or actual purchase. For example, a client may commission an interior decorator to redo her house, and we may entrust a broker to make crucial buy/sell decisions on our behalf. Marketers tend to overlook surrogates when they try to convince consumers to buy their goods or services. This can be a big mistake, because they may mistarget their communications to end consumers instead of to the surrogates who actually sift through product information and decide among product alternatives on their behalf.

> Regardless of whether they actually make the purchase on behalf of the consumer, surrogates' recommendations can be enormously influential.

TRUTH

37

Hundreds of housewives can predict your company's future

Are all of us smarter than any of us? A *prediction market* is one of the hottest new trends in forecasting the future. This approach asserts that groups of people with knowledge about an industry are jointly better predictors of the future than are any individuals—especially when each person stands to benefit from picking winners, just as they would if they were choosing companies to invest in on the New York Stock Exchange.

Companies from Microsoft to Eli Lilly and Hewlett-Packard empower their employees as "traders" who place bets on what they think will happen regarding future sales, the success of new products, or how other firms in a distribution channel will behave. For example, the pharmaceutical giant Eli Lilly routinely places multimillion-dollar bets on drug candidates that face overwhelming odds of failure—the relatively few new compounds that do succeed need to make enough money to cover the losses that the others incur. Obviously, the company will benefit if it can do a better job of separating the winners from the losers earlier in the process. Lilly ran an experiment where about 50 of its employees involved in drug development, including chemists, biologists, and project managers, traded six mock drug candidates through an internal market. The group correctly predicted the three most successful drugs.[58]

> A prediction market is one of the hottest new trends in forecasting the future.

In another emerging application, many companies are finding that it's both cost efficient and productive to call on outsiders from around the world to solve problems that their own scientists can't handle. Just as a firm might outsource production to a subcontractor, these companies are *crowdsourcing*. For example, InnoCentive is a network of more than 90,000 "solvers" that member companies, such as Boeing, DuPont, Procter & Gamble, and Eli Lilly, invite to tackle problems they are wrestling with internally. If a "solver" finds a solution, he or she gets a $10,000 to $100,000 reward.

38

Know who wears the pants in the family

The decision process within a household unit resembles a business conference. Certain matters go on the table for discussion, different members have different priorities and agendas, and there may be power struggles to rival any tale of corporate intrigue.

So, who "wears the pants" in the family? Sometimes it's not obvious which spouse makes the decisions. Indeed, although many men still wear the pants, it's women who buy them. When Haggar's research showed that nearly half of married women bought pants for their husbands without them being present, the firm started advertising its menswear products in women's magazines.[59]

Figuring out who makes buying decisions in a family is an important issue for marketers, because this information tells them who to target and whether they need to reach both spouses to influence a choice. For example, marketing research in the 1950s indicated that women were beginning to play a larger role in household purchasing decisions. In response, lawn mower manufacturers began to emphasize the rotary mower over other power mowers to downplay women's fears of injury.

In traditional families (and especially those with low educational levels), women are primarily responsible for family financial management—the man makes it, and the woman spends it. Each spouse "specializes" in certain activities. The pattern is different among families where more modern

> Figuring out who makes buying decisions in a family is an important issue for marketers.

sex-role norms operate. These couples believe both people should participate in family maintenance activities. In these cases, husbands assume more responsibility for laundering, housecleaning, grocery shopping, and so on, in addition to such traditionally "male" tasks as home maintenance and garbage removal. Shared decision making is becoming the norm for most American couples today—a Roper poll reported that 94 percent of partnered women say they make the decision or share equally in home furnishings selections (not a huge surprise), but in addition, 81 percent said the same for financial savings/investments, and 74 percent participate in deciding what car to buy.[60]

As Hallmark well knows, women across the social spectrum still are primarily responsible for the continuation of the family's *kin-network system*: They perform the rituals that maintain ties among family members, both immediate and extended. Women are more likely to coordinate visits among relatives, stay in touch with family members, send greeting cards, and arrange social engagements. This organizing role means that women often make important decisions about the family's leisure activities, and they are more likely to decide with whom the family will socialize.

Shared decision making is becoming the norm for most American couples today.

TRUTH

39

Youth is wasted on the young

Carmakers are wooing a new kind of consumer: one who's too young to drive. Many are advertising in child-oriented areas such as gyms that cater to kids, social networking sites where young people hang out, and the Saturday morning cartoons. In Whyville.net, a digital world where nearly two million children aged 8 to 15 hang out, kids can buy virtual Scion xBs if they have enough "clams" (Whyville's monetary unit). If not, they can meet with Eric, a virtual Toyota Financial Services adviser, to finance an xB replica they can use to tool around while in-world. Why bother pushing cars on kids? That's easy: About one-third of parents say their children "actively participate" in car-buying decisions.

Young consumers make up three distinct markets:

> About one-third of parents say their children "actively participate" in car-buying decisions.

- **Primary market**—Kids spend a lot on their own wants and needs that include toys, apparel, movies, and games. When marketers at M&Ms candy figured out who was actually buying a lot of their products, they redesigned vending machines with coin slots lower to the ground to accommodate shorter people, and sales rose dramatically. Most children choose their own brands of toothpaste, shampoo, and adhesive bandage. A large survey of kids aged 6 to 11 also revealed these tidbits:[61]

  - Seven percent have visited or used MySpace.com in the past month.

  - Ten percent have downloaded music online in the past month.

  - Six percent have written or read an online journal or blog in the past month.

  - Fifty-four percent have televisions in their rooms.

  - Twenty-six percent have stereos in their rooms.

  - Nineteen percent have computers in their rooms.

■ **Influence market**—*Parental yielding* is the polite way to describe what occurs when a parent "surrenders" to a child's request. Yielding drives many product selections, because about 90 percent of requests to a parent are by brand name. Researchers estimate that children directly influence about $453 billion worth of family purchases in a year. They report that, on average, children weigh in with a purchase request every 2 minutes when they shop with parents.[62] In recognition of this influence, Mrs. Butterworth's Syrup created a $6 million campaign to target kids directly with humorous ads that show the lengths to which adults will go to get the syrup bottle to talk to them. An executive who worked on the campaign explained, "We needed to create the *nag factor* [where kids demand their parents buy the product]."[63]

> Researchers estimate that children directly influence about $453 billion worth of family purchases in a year.

■ **Future market**—Kids have a way of growing up to be adults, so savvy marketers try to lock in brand loyalty at an early age. That explains why Kodak encourages kids to become photographers. Currently, only 20 percent of children aged 5 to 12 own cameras, and they shoot an average of only one roll of film a year. The company produces ads that portray photography as a cool pursuit and as a form of rebellion. It packages cameras with an envelope to mail the film directly back so parents can't see the photos.

TRUTH

40

Make millions on Millennials

In 1956, the label "teenage" entered the general American vocabulary when Frankie Lymon and the Teenagers became the first pop group to identify themselves with this new subculture. Believe it or not, the concept of a teenager is a fairly new idea. Throughout most of history, a person simply made the transition from child to adult, and many cultures marked this abrupt change in status with some sort of ritual or ceremony.

So-called Generation Y kids go by several names, including "Echo Boomers" and "Millennials." They already make up nearly one-third of the U.S. population, and they spend $170 billion a year of their own and their parents' money. They love brands like Sony, Patagonia, Gap, Aveda, and Apple. Echo Boomers are the most diverse generation ever. Thirty-five percent are nonwhite, and many grow up in nontraditional families. Today, one in four 21-year-olds was raised by a single parent, and three out of four have a working mother.

Unlike their parents or older siblings, Gen Y-ers tend to hold relatively traditional values, and they believe in the value of fitting in rather than rebelling. Their upbringing has stressed teamwork—team teaching, team grading, collaborative sports, community service, service learning, and student juries. Violent crime among teenagers is down 60 percent to 70 percent. The use of tobacco and alcohol is at an all-time low, as is teen pregnancy. Five out of ten Echo Boomers say they trust the government, and virtually all of them trust Mom and Dad.[64]

> Unlike their parents or older siblings, Gen Y-ers tend to hold relatively traditional values, and they believe in the value of fitting in rather than rebelling.

Millennials are the first generation to grow up with computers at home, in a 500-channel TV universe. They are multitaskers with cell phones, music downloads, and instant messaging on the Internet. They are totally at home in a *thumb culture* that communicates online and by cell phone (more likely via text and IM than by voice). These consumers truly are *digital natives*. Many young people prefer to use the Internet to communicate because its anonymity makes it easier to talk to people of the opposite sex or of different ethnic and racial groups.

Young consumers think that wired phones or computers are antiques. They're jugglers who value being both footloose and connected to

They are totally at home in a *thumb culture* that communicates online and by cell phone (more likely via text and IM than by voice).

their "peeps" 24/7. The advertising agency Saatchi & Saatchi labels this new kind of lifestyle *connexity*. When Toyota was developing its youth-oriented Scion model, its researchers learned that Echo Boomers practically live in their cars; one-quarter of Gen Y-ers, for example, keep a full change of clothes in their vehicles. So Toyota's designers made the Scion resemble a home on wheels: It has fully reclining front seats so that drivers can nap between classes and a 15-volt outlet so that they can plug in their computers.

One pair of researchers took an in-depth look at how 13- and 14-year-olds integrate the computer into their lives and how they use it to express their *cyberidentities*. These tweens have limited mobility in real life (too young to drive), so they use the computer to transport themselves to other places and modes of being. The researchers explored the metaphors these kids use when they think about their computers. For some, the PC is a "fraternity house" where they can socialize; it also can be a "carnival" where they play games and an "external brain" that helps with homework.[65] Clearly, young people are forging intimate relationships with these portals to online spaces we are only beginning to understand.

Because modern teens were raised on TV and tend to be more "savvy" than older generations, marketers must tread lightly in attempts to reach them. In particular, Gen Y-ers must see the messages as authentic and not condescending. So, what are the rules of engagement for young consumers?

- **Rule 1:** Don't talk down—Younger consumers want to feel they are drawing their own conclusions about products. In the words of one teen: "I don't like it when someone tells me what to do. Those drug and sex commercials preach. What do they know? Also, I don't like it when they show a big party and say, 'Come on and fit in with this product.' That's not how it works."

- **Rule 2:** Don't try to be what you're not. Stay true to your brand image—Kids value straight talk. Firms that back up what they say impress them. Procter & Gamble appealed to this value with a money-back guarantee on its Old Spice High Endurance deodorant with an invitation to phone 1-800-PROVEIT.

- **Rule 3:** Entertain them. Make it interactive and keep the sell short—Gen Y kids like to find brands in unexpected places. The prospect of catching appealing ads is part of the reason they're watching that TV show in the first place. If they want to learn more, they'll check out your Web site.

- **Rule 4:** Show that you know what they're going through, but keep it light—A commercial for Hershey's Ice Breakers mints subtly points out its benefit when it highlights the stress a guy feels as he's psyching himself up to approach a strange girl at a club. "I'm wearing my lucky boxers," he reassures himself. "Don't trip. Don't drool. Relax. How's my breath?"

TRUTH

41

Grownups don't grow up anymore

Restylane is the top-selling dermal injection to reduce the appearance of wrinkles. In 2007 the company decided to pitch it directly to consumers for the first time so, in keeping with new media trends, it launched a multipronged campaign that recognized the technical prowess of many middle-aged people. A conventional TV spot features before-and-after results, along with women who talk about how frequently men check them out after the treatment. But a second component is a video skit on YouTube that supposedly takes place during a woman's fiftieth birthday party. While her son works on a video birthday card, Mom gets caught smooching with a younger man on a couch. Viewers don't know the skit is an ad until the last 15 seconds. A third prong is a contest to name the "Hottest Mom in America"; contestants will submit videos to a Web site, and the winner gets cash, free treatments for a year, and an interview with a modeling agency. Today's Mom isn't exactly June Cleaver.

The baby boomer age cohort (people born between 1946 and 1964) consists of people whose parents established families following the end of World War II and during the 1950s when the peacetime economy was strong and stable. (As a general rule, when people feel confident about how things are going in the world, they are more likely to decide to have children.) As teenagers in the 1960s and 1970s, the "Woodstock generation" created a revolution in style, politics, and consumer attitudes. As they have aged, they have fueled cultural events as diverse as the Free Speech movement and hippies in the 1960s to Reaganomics and yuppies in the 1980s. Now that they are older, they continue to influence popular culture.

Today's Mom isn't exactly June Cleaver.

As the Restalyne campaign demonstrates, this generation is much more active and physically fit than its predecessors, and they're now in their peak earning years. As one commercial for VH1, the music video network that caters to those who are a bit too old for MTV, pointed out, "The generation that dropped acid to escape reality...is the generation that drops antacid to cope with it."

Levi Strauss is a good example of a company that has built its core business on the backs (or backsides) of boomers. More recently, though, the apparel maker faced the challenge of keeping aging customers in its franchise as former jeans-wearing hippies lost interest in traditional styles. Levi Strauss answered this challenge when it created its "New Casuals" product category with pants that are more formal than jeans but more casual than dress slacks. The target audience is men aged 25 to 49 with higher-than-average education and income, who work in white-collar jobs in major metropolitan areas. The Dockers line was born.

Consumers aged 35 to 44 spend the most on housing, cars, and entertainment. Baby boomers are busy "feathering their nests"; they account for roughly 40 percent of all the money consumers spend on household furnishings and equipment. In addition, consumers aged 45 to 54 spend the most of any age category on food (30 percent above average), apparel (38 percent above average), and retirement programs (57 percent above average).[66] To appreciate the impact that middle-aged consumers have and will have on our economy, consider this: At current spending levels, a one percent increase in the population of householders aged 35 to 54 results in an additional $8.9 billion in consumer spending.

In addition to the direct demand for products and services that this age group creates, these consumers have fostered a new baby boom of their own to keep marketers busy in the future. Because fertility rates have dropped, this new boom is not as big as the one that created the baby boom generation; we can best describe the new upsurge in the number of children as a *baby boomlet*. Many boomer couples postponed getting married and having children because of the new opportunities and options for women. They began having babies in their late 20s and early 30s, resulting in fewer (but perhaps more pampered) children per family. This new emphasis on children and the family creates opportunities for products such as cars (the success of the SUV concept among "soccer Moms"), services (the day-care industry and big chains such as KinderCare), and media (magazines such as *Working Mother*).

Although advertisers are always lured by youth, many are reconsidering this fixation in light of boomers' huge spending power.

Although advertisers are always lured by youth, many are reconsidering this fixation in light of boomers' huge spending power.

An ad for the Toyota Highlander, which shows boomers whose nests are emptying, declares, "For your newfound freedom, it's about how you are going to reinvent yourself for what could be 30 or 40 years of retirement, which is very different from your parents and grandparents." Even mobile marketers who typically blast messages to kids on their cell phones are beginning to target the middle-aged. For example, *Redbook* readers can bid on a year's worth of movie tickets via text messaging.

TRUTH

42

Dollar stores make good cents

About 14 percent of Americans live below the poverty line, and most marketers largely ignore this segment. Still, although poor people obviously have less to spend than do rich ones, they have the same basic needs as everyone else. Low-income families purchase staples, such as milk, orange juice, and tea, at the same rates as average-income families. Minimum wage–level households spend more than average on out-of-pocket health-care costs, rent, and food they eat at home. Unfortunately, they find it harder to obtain these resources because many businesses are reluctant to locate in lower-income areas. On average, residents of poor neighborhoods must travel more than 2 miles to have the same access to supermarkets, large drugstores, and banks as do residents of more affluent areas.

Still, a lot of companies are taking a second look at marketing to the poor because of their large numbers. The economist C. K. Pralahad added fuel to this fire with his book *The Fortune at the Bottom of the Pyramid*, which argued that big companies could profit and help the world's four billion poor or low-income people by finding innovative ways to sell them soap and refrigerators.

Low-income families purchase staples, such as milk, orange juice, and tea, at the same rates as average-income families.

Some companies are getting into these vast markets by revamping their distribution systems or making their products simpler and less expensive. When Nestlé Brazil shrank the package size of its Bono cookies (no relation to the U2 singer) from 200 grams to 140 grams and dropped the price, sales jumped 40 percent. Unilever called a new soap brand Ala so that illiterate people in Latin America could easily recognize it. In Mexico, the giant Cemex cement company improved housing in poor areas after it introduced a pay-as-you-go system for buying building supplies.

Muhammad Yunus, a Bangladeshi economist, won the 2006 Nobel Prize in Economics for pioneering the concept of *microloans*.

His Grameen Bank loans small sums—typically less than $100—to entrepreneurs in developing countries. Many of these go to "cell-phone women," who rent time on the phones to others in their remote villages. The bank has issued about six million loans to date, and almost 99 percent of recipients repay them (compared to a 50 percent repayment rate for a typical bank in a developing country).

The success of La Curacao, a chain of department stores in southern California with a Hispanic focus, comes from the company's desire to serve the needs of lower-income consumers. The stores are the brainchild of two Israeli brothers who share a similar experience with many of their customers: They were once illegal immigrants searching for a better life in the United States. They realized that poor people can be good credit risks, *if* the retailer gives them reason to be grateful that someone has taken a chance on them. This trust seems to be working: Shoppers use store credit cards for 95 percent of purchases, and for eight out of ten of these customers, the La Curacao credit card is the first one they've ever had. The chain's slogan is *Un Poco de Su Pais* or "A Little Bit of Your Country." Everything about the stores—from the exterior emblazoned with Mayan and Aztec statues to the piped-in salsa music, Spanish-speaking sales staff, and Spanish-language sale signs inside—strives to make the customers feel as if they're back home. And because many of the immigrant families who shop there can't afford to take their kids to places such as Disneyland, every store also has a stage that features mariachi bands, clowns, and other family entertainment.

> Poor people can be good credit risks.

TRUTH

43

The rich are different

If you've got enough Benjamins (translation for readers over age 25: $100 bills), you can buy a Pink Splendor Barbie complete with crystal jewelry and a bouffant gown sewn with 24-karat threads. To dress a "living doll," Victoria's Secret offers its Million Dollar Miracle Bra, with more than 100 carats of real diamonds.

Obviously, many companies love to sell to affluent, upscale markets. This focus often makes sense, because these consumers have the resources to spend on costly products (often with higher profit margins). However, it is a mistake to assume that we should place everyone with a high income into the same well-lined bucket. After all, social class involves a lot more than absolute income. It is also a way of life, and factors including where they got their money, how they got it, and how long they have had it significantly affect affluents' interests and spending priorities.

Despite our stereotype of rich people living it up, the typical millionaire is a 57-year-old man who is self-employed, earns a median household income of $131,000, has been married to the same wife for most of his adult life, has children, has never spent more than $399 on a suit or more than $140 for a pair of shoes, and drives a Ford Explorer. (The humble billionaire investor Warren Buffett comes to mind.) Interestingly, many affluent people don't consider themselves to be rich. One tendency researchers notice is that they indulge in luxury goods while pinching pennies on everyday items—buying shoes at Neiman Marcus and deodorant at Wal-Mart, for example.[67]

> It is a mistake to assume that we should place everyone with a high income into the same well-lined bucket.

To generalize, people who are used to having money use their fortunes a lot differently. Old money families (the Rockefellers, DuPonts, Fords, and so on) live primarily on inherited funds. Merely having wealth is not sufficient to achieve social prominence in these circles. You also need to demonstrate a family history of public service and philanthropy, and tangible markers of these contributions often enable donors to achieve a kind of immortality (Rockefeller

University, Carnegie Hall, or the Whitney Museum). "Old money" consumers distinguish among themselves in terms of ancestry and lineage rather than wealth. And, they're secure in their status: In a sense, they have trained their whole lives to be rich.

Pity the poor nouveau riches who actually earn their money; many suffer from *status anxiety*. They monitor the cultural environment to ensure that they do the "right" thing, wear the "right" clothes, get seen at the "right" places, use the "right" caterer, and so on. In major Chinese cities such as Shanghai, some people have taken to wearing pajamas in public as a way to flaunt their newfound wealth. As one consumer explained, "Only people in cities can afford clothes like this. In farming villages, they still have to wear old work clothes to bed."[68]

Nouveau or not, we all have a deep-seated tendency to evaluate ourselves, our professional accomplishments, our appearance, and our material well-being relative to others. The rise of a *mass-class* market means that many luxury products have gone down-market; once-exclusive designer names appear on the bodies, homes, and garages of many consumers who used to only look at them longingly in magazines or on *Lifestyles of the Rich and Famous*. Does this mean we no longer yearn for status symbols? Hardly. The market continues to roll out ever-pricier goods and services, from $130,000 Hummers and $12,000 mother-baby diamond tennis bracelet sets to $600 jeans, $800 haircuts, and $400 bottles of wine. Although it seems that almost everyone can flout a designer handbag (or at least a counterfeit version with a convincing logo), our country's wealthiest consumers employ 9,000 personal chefs, visit plastic surgeons, and send their children to $400-an-hour math tutors.

> The rise of a *mass-class* market means that many luxury products have gone down-market.

The social analyst Thorstein Veblen first discussed the motivation to consume for the sake of consuming at the turn of the twentieth century. For Veblen, we buy things to inspire envy in others through our display of wealth or power. Veblen coined the term *conspicuous consumption* to refer to people's desires to provide prominent visible evidence of their ability

171

to afford luxury goods. The material excesses of his time motivated Veblen's outlook; he wrote in the era of the "Robber Barons," where the likes of J. P. Morgan, Henry Clay Frick, and William Vanderbilt built massive financial empires and flaunted their wealth as they competed to throw the most lavish party.

Sounds like they really lived it up back in the old days, right? Well, maybe the more things change, the more they stay the same: The recent wave of corporate scandals involving companies such as Enron, WorldCom, and Tyco infuriated many consumers when they discovered that some top executives lived it up even as other employees were laid off. One account of a $1 million birthday party that the chief executive of Tyco threw for his wife is eerily similar to a robber baron shindig: The party reportedly had a gladiator theme and featured an ice sculpture of Michelangelo's David with vodka streaming from his penis into crystal glasses.

The rich *are* different.

TRUTH

44

Out with the ketchup, in with the salsa

Marketers cannot ignore the stunning diversity of cultures that are reshaping mainstream society. Ethnic minorities spend more than $600 billion a year on products and services, so firms must tailor products and communications strategies to their unique needs. Immigrants now make up 10 percent of the U.S. population and will account for 13 percent by 2050.

This important change encourages advertisers to rethink their old strategies, which assumed that virtually all of their customers were Caucasians hailing from Western Europe. For example, as part of Crest toothpaste's fiftieth-anniversary celebration, Procter & Gamble revived its "Crest Kid," who first appeared as an apple-cheeked urchin that Norman Rockwell illustrated in 1956. Now, a Cuban-born girl plays the character. Although some people feel uncomfortable with the notion that marketers should explicitly take into account people's racial and ethnic differences when they formulate their strategies, the reality is that these subcultural memberships do shape many consumers' needs and wants. Research indicates, for example, that members of minority groups find an advertising spokesperson from their own group more trustworthy, and this enhanced credibility in turn translates into more positive brand attitudes. However, marketers need to avoid the pitfall of painting all members of an ethnic or racial group with the same brush; these generalizations not only are inaccurate, but they also are likely to turn off the very people a company wants to reach.

Ethnic marketing is in vogue with many firms, but actually defining and targeting members of a distinct ethnic group is not always so easy in our "melting pot" society. In the 2000 U.S. Census, some 7 million people identified with two or more races, refusing to describe themselves as only white, black, Asian, Korean, Samoan, or one of the other racial categories. The popularity of

> Ethnic minorities spend more than $600 billion a year on products and services, so firms must tailor products and communications strategies to their unique needs.

golfer Tiger Woods illuminates the complexity of ethnic identity in the United States. Although we laud Tiger as an African American role model, in reality he is a model of multiracialism. His mother is Thai, and he also has Caucasian and Indian ancestry. Other popular multiracial celebrities include actor Keanu Reeves (Hawaiian, Chinese, and Caucasian), singer Mariah Carey (black Venezuelan and white), and Dean Cain of *Superman* fame (Japanese and Caucasian).

In the 2000 U.S. Census, some 7 million people identified with two or more races, refusing to describe themselves as only white, black, Asian, Korean, Samoan, or one of the other racial categories.

The bulk of American immigrants historically came from Europe, but immigration patterns have shifted dramatically. New immigrants are much more likely to be Asian or Hispanic. As these new waves of immigrants settle in the United States, marketers try to track their consumption patterns and adjust their strategies accordingly. It's best to market to these new arrivals— whether Arabs, Asians, Russians, or people of Caribbean descent—in their native languages. They tend to cluster together geographically, which makes them easy to reach. The local community is the primary source for information and advice, so word of mouth is especially important.

In the past, marketers used ethnic symbolism as shorthand to convey certain product attributes. They often employed crude and unflattering images when they depicted African Americans as subservient or Mexicans as bandits. Aunt Jemima sold pancake mix, and Rastus was a grinning black chef who pitched Cream of Wheat hot cereal. The Gold Dust Twins were black urchins who peddled a soap powder for Lever Brothers, and Pillsbury hawked powdered drink mixes using characters such as Injun Orange and Chinese Cherry—who had buck teeth. As the Civil Rights Movement gave more power to minority groups and their rising economic status began to command marketers' respect, these negative stereotypes began to disappear. Frito-Lay responded to protests by the Hispanic community and stopped using the Frito Bandito character in 1971, and Quaker Foods gave Aunt Jemima a makeover in 1989.

Now, the Mars company is taking an interesting risk with its Uncle Ben's rice brand. For more than 60 years, packages featured the black Uncle Ben character. He wore a bow tie evocative of servants and Pullman porters, and his title reflects how white Southerners once used "uncle" and "aunt" as honorary names for older African Americans because the whites refused to call the African Americans "Mr." and "Mrs." Mars is reviving the character, but he's been remade as Ben, an accomplished businessman with an opulent office who shares his "grains of wisdom" about rice and life on the brand's Web site.

TRUTH

45

Look for fly-fishing born-again environmentalist jazz-loving Harry Potter freaks

Our group memberships within our society-at-large define us. A *subculture* is a group whose members share beliefs and common experiences that set them apart from others. Every one of us belongs to many subcultures, depending on our age, race, ethnic background, or place of residence.

The staggering diversity of consumers' interests and activities today means that it's usually no longer meaningful to speak of a mass market. We are witnessing a continuing spiral of *market fragmentation* that requires us to speak with increasingly greater precision to smaller groups of consumers—but the upside is that we can focus our messages very sharply to reach them.

In contrast to larger, demographically based subcultures like Hispanic-Americans or baby boomers (that Nature usually determines), people who are part of a *microculture* freely choose to identify with a lifestyle or aesthetic preference. A good example is the microculture that automobile hobbyists call "Tuners." These are single men in their late teens and early 20s, usually in Latino or Asian communities, who share a passion for fast cars, high-tech auto upgrades, and specialized car parts. This microculture started with late night meets among illegal street racers in New York and L.A. Now, Tuners are more mainstream; magazines including *Import Tuner* and *Sport Compact Car* and major companies such as Pioneer eagerly court these high-tech hot-rodders. A commercial for the Honda Civic aimed straight for Tuners; it showed a fleet of cars sporting customized features such as chrome rims and tinted windows.

> We are witnessing a continuing spiral of *market fragmentation* that requires us to speak with increasingly greater precision to smaller groups of consumers.

Whether Tuners, Dead Heads, or skinheads, each microculture exhibits its own unique set of norms, vocabulary, and product insignias (think of the Grateful Dead subculture's distinctive skull and roses). A study of contemporary "mountain men" in the western United States illustrates the binding influence of a microculture on its members. Researchers found that group members shared a strong sense of identity that they expressed in weekend retreats, where they reinforced these ties by using authentic items like tepees, buffalo robes, buckskin leggings, and beaded moccasins to create a sense of community among fellow mountain men.

These microcultures can even gel around fictional characters and events, and they often play a key role in defining our self-concept. Many devotees of *Star Trek*, for example, immerse themselves in a make-believe world of starships, phasers, and Vulcan mind melds. Our microcultures typically command fierce loyalty: *Star Trek* fans are notorious for their devotion to the cause, as this excerpt from a fan's email illustrates:

> I have to admit to keeping pretty quiet about my devotion to the show for many years simply because people do tend to view a *Trek* fan as weird or crazy...[after attending her first convention she says:] Since then I have proudly worn my Bajoran earring and not cared about the looks I get from others.... I have also met...other Trek fans, and some of these people have become very close friends. We have a lot in common and have had some of the same experiences as concerns our love of *Trek*.[69]

Star Trek is a merchandising empire that continues to beam up millions of dollars in revenues. Needless to say, it's not alone in this regard. Numerous other microcultures are out there, thriving on their collective worship of mythical and not-so-mythical worlds and characters ranging from the music group Phish to Hello Kitty. Indeed, it's fascinating to realize just how many microcultures are out there (often reinforced by our obsession with blogging about anything and everything that we experience) and the products they can coalesce around. Consider, for example, the devotion to Peeps; every year people buy about 1.5 billion of these mostly tasteless marshmallow chicks; about two-thirds of them sell around Easter. They have no nutritional value, but they do have a shelf life of two

It's fascinating to realize just how many microcultures are out there (often reinforced by our obsession with blogging about anything and everything that we experience) and the products they can coalesce around.

years. Maybe that's why not all Peeps get eaten. Devotees use them in decorations, dioramas, online slide shows, and sculptures. Some fans feel challenged to test their physical properties: On more than 200 Peeps Web sites, you can see fetishists skewering, microwaving, hammering, decapitating, and otherwise abusing the spongy confections.

If a homely marshmallow candy can attain icon status in a microculture, might your product be next?

TRUTH

46

Ronald McDonald is related to Luke Skywalker

A *myth* is a story with symbolic elements that represents a culture's ideals.

Consider, for example, a familiar story in our culture: *Little Red Riding Hood*. This myth started as a peasants' tale in sixteenth-century France, where a girl meets a werewolf on her way to granny's house. (There is historical evidence for a plague of wolf attacks during this time, including several incidents where men were tried for allegedly transforming themselves into the deadly animals.) The werewolf has already killed granny, stored her flesh in the pantry, and poured her blood in a bottle. Contrary to the version we know, however, when the girl arrives at the house, she snacks on granny, strips naked, and climbs into bed with the wolf! To make the story even more scandalous, some versions refer to the wolf as a "gaffer" (a contraction of "grandfather"), implying incest as well.

This story first appeared in print in 1697 as a warning to the loose ladies of Louis XIV's court. (The author puts her in red in this version, because this color symbolizes harlots.) Eventually, the Brothers Grimm wrote their own version in 1812, but they substituted violence for sex to scare kids into behaving. And, to reinforce the sex-role standards of that time, in the Grimm version, a man rescues the girl from the wolf. So, this myth sends vivid messages about such cultural no-nos as cannibalism, incest, and promiscuity.

An understanding of cultural myths is important to marketers who, in some cases (most likely unconsciously), pattern their messages along a mythic structure. Consider, for example, the way that McDonald's takes on "mythical" qualities. The "golden arches" are a symbol that consumers everywhere recognize as virtually synonymous with American culture. They offer sanctuary to Americans around the world; Americans know exactly what to expect once they enter. Basic struggles involving good versus evil play out in the fantasy world that McDonald's advertising creates, for example, when Ronald McDonald

An understanding of cultural myths is important to marketers who, in some cases (most likely unconsciously), pattern their messages along a mythic structure.

confounds the Hamburglar. McDonald's even has a "seminary" (Hamburger University) where inductees go to learn the Ways of The Golden Arches.

We associate myths with the ancient Greeks or Romans but, in reality, comic books, movies, holidays, and yes, even commercials embody our own cultural myths. Consider the popularity of the elaborate weddings that Disney stages for couples who want to reenact their own version of a popular fairy tale. At Disney World, the princess bride wears a tiara and rides to the park's lakeside wedding pavilion in a horse-drawn coach, complete with two footmen in gray wigs and gold lamé pants. At the exchange of vows, trumpets blare as Major Domo (he helped the Duke in his quest for Cinderella) walks up the aisle with two wedding bands gently placed in a glass slipper on a velvet pillow. Disney stages about 2,000 of these extravaganzas each year. Disney is expanding the appeal of this myth as it moves into the bridal gown business. It sells a line of billowing princess gowns complete with crystal tiaras. Fairy-tale brides can walk down the aisle posing as Cinderella, Snow White, Belle, Sleeping Beauty, Jasmine, or Ariel.

Comic book superheroes demonstrate how a culture communicates myths to consumers of all ages. Marvel Comics' Spiderman character tells stories about balancing the obligations of being a superhero with the

> We associate myths with the ancient Greeks or Romans but, in reality, comic books, movies, holidays, and yes, even commercials embody our own cultural myths.

need of his alter ego, Peter Parker, to succeed in school and have a normal love life. Indeed, some of these fictional figures embody such fundamental properties that they become a *monomyth*, a myth that is common to many cultures. Consider Superman; a father (Jor-El) gives his only son to save a world with his supernatural powers. Sound familiar?

TRUTH

47

Sign a caveman to endorse your product

People love the Geico caveman. He appeared in commercials as a throwback dressed in "yuppie" clothing who struggles against Geico's insensitivity when its ads claimed, "It's so easy even a caveman can do it." How much do viewers love him? Well, ABC decided to develop a sitcom (okay, a short-lived one) about a group of caveman roommates who battle prejudice in modern-day America. This nouveau Fred Flintstone isn't alone. Burger King's creepy "King" mascot shows up in a series of video games, and the fast-food chain is arranging for him to star in a feature film. And the mythical Simpsons family debuted in real life as 7-Eleven transformed many of its stores into Kwik-E-Marts to promote the cartoon series' movie. During the promotion, customers snapped up KrustyO's cereal, Buzz Cola, and ice Squishees, all products from the show.

Reality engineering occurs when marketers appropriate elements of popular culture and use them as promotional vehicles. Reality engineers have many tools at their disposal; they plant products in movies, pump scents into offices and stores, attach video monitors in the backs of taxicabs, buy ad space on police patrol cars, or film faked "documentaries" such as *The Blair Witch Project* and *Cloverfield*. A New York couple funded their $80,000 wedding by selling corporate plugs; they inserted coupons in their programs and tossed 25 bouquets from 1-800-FLOWERS. Internet casino GoldenPalace.com paid people a total of $100,000 to tattoo the company name on their foreheads, cleavage, and pregnant bellies. In one poll, about half of the respondents said they would consider accepting money from corporations in exchange for naming rights to their babies. Others do

Reality engineering occurs when marketers appropriate elements of popular culture and use them as promotional vehicles.

it for free: In 2000, the latest year for which data is available, 571 babies in the United States were named Armani, 55 were named Chevy, and 21 were named L'Oréal.

Many types of products play starring (or at least supporting) roles in our culture.

Traditionally, TV networks demanded that producers "geek" (alter) brand names before they could appear in a show, as when *Melrose Place* changed a Nokia cell phone to a "Nokio." Nowadays, though, real products pop up everywhere. A script for ABC's soap opera *All My Children* was reworked so that one of the characters would plug a new Wal-Mart perfume called Enchantment. Daytime TV stars eat Butterball turkeys, wear NASCAR shirts, and use Kleenex tissue. And the characters on the soap have been drinking a lot of Florida orange juice—not only because they're thirsty. *Product placement* is the insertion of real products in fictional movies, TV shows, books, and plays. Many types of products play starring (or at least supporting) roles in our culture; in 2007, for example, the most visible brands ranged from Coca-Cola and Nike apparel to the Chicago Bears football team and the Pussycat Dolls band.

For better or worse, products are popping up everywhere. Worldwide product placement in all media was worth $3.5 billion in 2004, a 200 percent increase from 1994. New advances in technology are taking product placement to the next level, as producers can insert brands into shows after filming them. Virtual product placement put a box of Club Crackers into an episode of *Yes, Dear*; producers also inserted Cheez-It crackers, a can of StarKist tuna, and Nutri-Grain bars into the show. This new procedure means that a brand doesn't have to be written into the script, and it can't be deleted by late editing changes.

Is the placement worth the effort? A 2006 study reported that consumers respond well to placements when the show's plot makes the product's benefit clear. It found that the year's most effective brand integration occurred on ABC's now-cancelled *Miracle Workers* reality show, where physicians performed novel, life-changing surgeries. Audiences reacted strongly to CVS Pharmacy's role in covering the costs of medications that patients needed after the procedures.

TRUTH

48

Make your brand a fortress brand—and make mine a Guinness

A *ritual* is a set of multiple, symbolic behaviors that occurs in a fixed sequence and is repeated periodically. Bizarre tribal ceremonies, perhaps involving animal or human sacrifice, may come to mind when you think of rituals but, in reality, many contemporary consumer activities are ritualistic.

Consider, for example, a ritual that many beer drinkers in the United Kingdom and Ireland hold near and dear to their hearts—the spectacle of a pub bartender "pulling" the perfect pint of Guinness. According to tradition, the slow pour takes exactly 119.5 seconds as the bartender holds the glass at a 45-degree angle, fills it three-quarters full, lets it settle, and tops it off with its signature creamy head. Guinness wanted to make the pull faster so that the bar could serve more drinks on a busy night, so it introduced FastPour, an ultrasound technology that dispenses the dark brew in only 25 seconds. Did you guess the outcome? The brewer had to scrap the system when drinkers resisted the innovation. You just don't mess with consumers' rituals.

> Bizarre tribal ceremonies, perhaps involving animal or human sacrifice, may come to mind when you think of rituals but, in reality, many contemporary consumer activities are ritualistic.

The BBDO Worldwide advertising agency labels brands that we closely link to our rituals *fortress brands* because, once they become embedded in our rituals—whether brushing our teeth, drinking a beer, or shaving—we're unlikely to replace them. The agency reported that people it observed in 26 countries practice some rituals in common, including one it labels *preparing for battle*. For most of us, this ritual means getting ready for work. Relevant activities include brushing our teeth, taking a shower or bath, having something to eat or drink, talking to a family member or partner, checking e-mail, shaving, putting on makeup, watching TV or listening to the radio, and reading a newspaper. The study claims that 89 percent of people use the same brands for these sequenced rituals, and three out of four are disappointed or irritated when something disrupts their ritual or their brand of choice isn't available.

Rituals occur at several levels. Public rituals such as the Super Bowl, presidential inaugurations, and graduation ceremonies are communal activities that affirm our membership in the larger group and reassure us that we are reading from the same script as everyone else. Other rituals occur in small groups or even in isolation. Market researchers discovered that, for many people, the act of late-night ice cream eating has ritualistic elements, often involving a favorite spoon and bowl! And rituals are not always set in stone; they change with the times. For example, when we throw rice at a wedding, we are expressing our desire for the couple to be fertile. In recent years, many newlyweds have substituted soap bubbles, jingling bells, or butterflies for the rice, because birds eat the rice, which expands inside their bodies with nasty results.

Many businesses owe their livelihoods to their ability to supply ritual artifacts to consumers.

Many businesses owe their livelihoods to their capability to supply *ritual artifacts* to consumers. These are items we need to perform rituals, such as wedding rice, birthday candles, diplomas, specialized foods and beverages (for example, wedding cakes, ceremonial wine, or even hot dogs at the ball park), trophies and plaques, band uniforms, greeting cards, and retirement watches. In addition, we often follow a ritual script to identify the artifacts we need, the sequence in which we should use them, and who uses them. Examples include graduation programs, fraternity manuals, and etiquette books. Make your brand a fortress brand.

TRUTH

49

Turn a (pet) rock into gold

In the early 1980s, Cabbage Patch dolls were all the rage among American children. Faced with a limited supply of the product, some retailers reported near-riots among adults as they tried desperately to buy the dolls for their children. A Milwaukee DJ jokingly announced that people should bring catcher's mitts to a local stadium, because an airplane was going to fly overhead and drop 2,000 dolls. He told his listeners to hold up their American Express cards so their numbers could be photographed from the plane. More than two dozen anxious parents apparently didn't get the joke; they showed up in subzero weather, mitts in hand.

The Cabbage Patch craze lasted for a couple of seasons before it eventually died out, and consumers moved on to other things, such as Teenage Mutant Ninja Turtles, which grossed more than $600 million in 1989. The Mighty Morphin Power Rangers eventually replaced the Turtles, and Beanie Babies and Giga Pets, in turn, deposed them before the invasion of Pokémon followed by Yu-Gi-Oh! cards and now Webkinz. What will be next?

Although the longevity of a particular style can range from a month to a century, fashions tend to flow in a predictable sequence. Like a person, an item or idea progresses through basic stages from birth to death. The fashion acceptance cycle is pretty predictable, but the rate at which it occurs is speeding up dramatically in our global and high-tech economy. This means that companies have to work harder than ever to continually innovate rather than simply introduce a great product and rest on their laurels. Product development cycles accelerate in many industries from apparel (which used to have four seasons but now has six per year) to computers.

> Although the longevity of a particular style can range from a month to a century, fashions tend to flow in a predictable sequence.

We distinguish among products in terms of the length of their acceptance cycle. A classic is a fashion with an extremely long acceptance cycle. It is, in a sense, "antifashion" because it guarantees stability and low risk to the purchaser for a long period. Keds sneakers, introduced in 1917, appeal to those who are turned off by the high fashion, trendy appeal of Nike or Reebok. When researchers asked consumers in focus groups to imagine what kind of building Keds would be, a common response was a country house with a white picket fence. In other words, consumers see the shoes as a stable, classic product. In contrast, participants described Nikes as steel-and-glass skyscrapers, reflecting their more modern image.

In contrast, a *fad* is a short-lived fashion. Relatively few people adopt a fad product. Adopters may all belong to a common subculture, and the fad "trickles across" members but rarely breaks out of that specific group. Indeed, others are likely to ridicule the fad (which may add fuel to the fire). Some notable past fad products include hula hoops, snap bracelets, and pet rocks. More recently, an entrepreneur named Johnny Earle caught the fad wave by turning his nickname—"Cupcake"—into a booming business. He started selling his T-shirts featuring cupcakes in unlikely situations (for example, one with a cupcake and crossbones) out of the trunk of his car. He wound up with two retail stores, including one on upscale Newbury Street in Boston. Customers walk away with the shirts wrapped in doughnut boxes rather than bags.

The first company to identify a trend and act on it has an advantage, whether the firm is Starbucks (gourmet coffee), Nabisco (Snackwells low-fat cookies and crackers), Taco Bell (value pricing), or Chrysler (retro cars). Nothing is certain, but some guidelines help to predict whether the innovation will endure as a long-term trend or if it's just a fad destined to go the way of hula-hoops, pet rocks, and little rubber spiders called Wally Wallwalkers that slowly crawled down walls instead of just dropping to the ground:

> The first company to identify a trend and act on it has an advantage.

- **Does it fit with basic lifestyle changes?** If a new hairstyle is hard to care for, this innovation isn't consistent with women's increasing time demands. However, the movement to shorter-term vacations is more likely to last, because this innovation makes trip planning easier for harried consumers who want to get away for a few days at a time.

- **What are the benefits?** The switch to poultry and fish from beef came about because these meats are healthier.

- **Can it be personalized?** Enduring trends tend to accommodate a desire for individuality, whereas styles such as Mohawk haircuts or the grunge look tend to lock followers in to a fairly restricted set of styles.

- **Is it a real trend or just a side effect of something else?** An increased interest in exercise is part of a basic trend toward health consciousness, although the specific form of exercise that is "in" at any given time will vary (for example, low-impact aerobics versus Pilates).

- **What other changes are occurring in the market?** Sometimes *carryover effects* influence the popularity of related products. The miniskirt fad in the 1960s boosted hosiery purchases substantially. Now, sales of these items are in decline because of today's more casual styles.

- **Who has adopted it?** If working mothers, baby boomers, or some other important market segment don't adopt the innovation, it is not likely to become a longer-term trend.

TRUTH
50

Think globally, act locally

When Wal-Mart started to open stores abroad in the early 1990s, it offered a little piece of America to foreign consumers—and that was the problem. The retail behemoth promoted golf clubs in soccer-mad Brazil and pushed ice skates in Mexico. It trained its German clerks to smile at customers—who thought they were flirting. Now Wal-Mart is adapting (though not in Germany—the company had to throw in the towel there). Its Chinese stores sell live turtles and snakes and lure shoppers who come on foot or bicycle with free shuttle buses and home delivery for refrigerators and other large items.

As corporations compete in many markets around the world, the debate intensifies regarding the need to develop separate marketing plans for each culture versus crafting a single plan that a firm implements everywhere. Let's briefly consider each viewpoint.

- **Adopt a standardized strategy**—Proponents of a standardized marketing strategy argue that many cultures, especially those of industrialized countries, have become so homogenized that the same approach will work throughout the world. By developing one approach for multiple markets, a company can benefit from economies of scale because it does not have to incur the substantial time and expense to develop a separate strategy for each culture. For example, Starbucks is becoming a household name in Japan (where it is pronounced *STAH-buks-zu*). Like their American counterparts, local Japanese outlets feature comfortable sofas, and hip-hop and reggae tunes play in the background.

- **Adopt a localized strategy**—Disney learned the hard way about the importance of being sensitive to local cultures after it opened its Euro Disney Park in 1992. The company got slammed for creating an entertainment venue that re-created its American locations without catering to local customs (such as serving wine with meals). Visitors to Euro Disney from many countries took offense, even at what seemed to be small slights—such as the sin of serving only French sausage to Germans, Italians, and others who believed their own local version to be superior. Disney applied the lessons it learned in cultural sensitivity to its newer Hong Kong Disneyland. Executives shifted the angle of the front gate by 12 degrees after they consulted a *feng shui* specialist, who said the change would ensure prosperity for the park. Cash registers are close to corners or along walls to increase prosperity. The company burned incense as it finished each building, and it picked a lucky day (September 12) for the opening. One of the park's main ballrooms measures 888 square meters because eight is a lucky number in Chinese culture.

In some cases, consumers in one place simply do not like some products that are popular elsewhere, or their different lifestyles require companies to adapt the way they make their products. IKEA finally realized that Americans use a lot of ice in their drinks, so they weren't buying smaller European glasses. The Swedish furniture chain also figured out that, compared to Europeans, Americans sleep in bigger beds, need bigger bookshelves, and like to curl up on sofas rather than sit on them. Snapple failed in Japan because the drink's cloudy appearance and the pulp floating in the bottles were a turnoff. Similarly, Frito-Lay stopped selling Ruffles potato chips (too salty) and Cheetos there. (The Japanese didn't appreciate having orange fingers after they ate a handful.) The company still makes Cheetos in China, but the local version doesn't contain cheese, which is not a staple of the Chinese diet. Instead, local flavors come in varieties such as Savory American Cream and Japanese Steak.

So, what's the verdict—does global marketing work? Perhaps the more appropriate question is, "When does it work?" Although the argument for a homogenous world culture is appealing in principle, in practice it hasn't worked out too well. One reason for the failure of global marketing is that consumers in different countries have varying conventions and customs, so they simply do not use products the same way. Kellogg, for example, discovered that, in Brazil, people don't typically eat a big breakfast— they're more likely to eat cereal as a dry snack.

> Although the argument for a homogenous world culture is appealing in principle, in practice it hasn't worked out too well.

Some large corporations such as Coca-Cola have been successful in crafting a single, international image. Still, even the soft drink giant must make minor modifications to the way it presents itself in each culture. Although Coke commercials are largely standardized, the company permits local agencies to edit them so that they highlight close-ups of local faces. To maximize the chances of success for these multicultural efforts, marketers must locate consumers in different countries who nonetheless share a common worldview. This is more likely to be the case among people whose frame of reference is relatively more international or cosmopolitan, or who receive much of their information about the world from sources that incorporate a worldwide perspective. The best candidates for standardization: affluent people who are "global citizens" and who come into contact with ideas from around the world through their travels, business contacts, and media experiences; and young people whose tastes in music and fashion are strongly influenced by MTV and other media that broadcast many of the same images to multiple countries.

> Young people whose tastes in music and fashion are strongly influenced by MTV and other media.

And that's the truth.

References

Truth 1

1 Kenji Hall, "Sony Walkman Wants the Spotlight Back," *BusinessWeek* (October 13, 2006), http://yahoo.businessweek. com/globalbiz/content/oct2006/gb20061013_132346.htm, accessed January 1, 2008.

Truth 2

2 Quoted in Jack Neff, "P&G Boosts Design's Role in Marketing," *Advertising Age* 1 no. 2 (February 9, 2004): 52.

Truth 3

3 Deborah J. Mitchell, Barbara E. Kahn, and Susan C. Knasko, "There's Something in the Air: Effects of Congruent or Incongruent Ambient Odor on Consumer Decision Making," *Journal of Consumer Research* 22 (September 1995): 229–38.

4 Maxine Wilkie, "Scent of a Market," *American Demographics* (August 1995): 40–49.

5 Nicholas Wade, "Scent of a Man Is Linked to a Woman's Selection," *New York Times Online* (January 22, 2002).

6 Nina M. Lentini, "KFC Targets the Nostrils of Hungry Office Workers" (August 29, 2007), *Marketing Daily*, www.mediapost.com. Accessed August 29, 2007.

Truth 4

7 Michael Lev, "No Hidden Meaning Here: Survey Sees Subliminal Ads," *New York Times* (May 3, 1991): D7.

Truth 5

8 Nicholas Bakalar (August 14, 2007), "If It Says McDonald's, Then It Must Be Good," *New York Times Online*, accessed August 14, 2007.

9 Albert H. Hastorf and Hadley Cantril, "They Saw a Game: A Case Study," *Journal of Abnormal and Social Psychology* 49 (1954): 129–134.

10 Benedict Carey, "Knowing the Ingredients Can Change the Taste," *New York Times Online* (December 12, 2006).

Truth 6

11 James Ward, Barbara Loken, Ivan Ross, and Tedi Hasapopoulous, "The Influence of Physical Similarity on Generalization of Affect and Attribute Perceptions from National Brands to Private Label Brands," in Terence A. Shimp et al., eds., *American Marketing Educators' Conference* (Chicago: American Marketing Association, 1986), 51–56.

Truth 7

12 Raymond R. Burke and Thomas K. Srull, "Competitive Interference and Consumer Memory for Advertising," *Journal of Consumer Research* 15 (June 1988): 55–68.

13 Rik G. M. Pieters and Tammo H. A. Bijmolt, "Consumer Memory for Television Advertising: A Field Study of Duration, Serial Position, and Competition Effects," *Journal of Consumer Research* 23 (March 1997): 362–372.

14 Erik Sass, "Study Finds Spectacular Print Ads Get Spectacular Recall," www.mediapost.com, February 23, 2007, accessed February 23, 2007.

15 Werner Krober-Riel, "Effects of Emotional Pictorial Elements in Ads Analyzed by Means of Eye Movement Monitoring," in Thomas C. Kinnear, ed., *Advances in Consumer Research* 11 (Provo, UT: Association for Consumer Research, 1984): 591–596.

16 Hans-Bernd Brosius, "Influence of Presentation Features and News Context on Learning from Television News," *Journal of Broadcasting & Electronic Media* 33 (Winter 1989): 1–14.

17 Edward F. McQuarrie and David Glen Mick, "Visual and Verbal Rhetorical Figures Under Directed Processing Versus Incidental Exposure to Advertising," *Journal of Consumer Research* (March 2003): 29, 579–587; cf. also Ann E. Schlosser, "Learning Through Virtual Product Experience: The Role of Imagery on True Versus False Memories," *Journal of Consumer Research* 33, no. 3 (2006): 377–383.

Truth 8

18 Keith Naughton and Bill Vlasic, "Nostalgia Boom," *BusinessWeek* (March 23, 1998): 59–64.

19 Robert M. Schindler and Morris B. Holbrook, "Nostalgia for Early Experience as a Determinant of Consumer Preferences," *Psychology & Marketing* 20, no. 4 (April 2003): 275–302; Morris B. Holbrook and Robert M. Schindler, "Some Exploratory Findings on the Development of Musical Tastes," *Journal of Consumer Research* 16 (June 1989): 119–124; Morris B. Holbrook and Robert M. Schindler, "Market Segmentation Based on Age and Attitude Toward the Past: Concepts, Methods, and Findings Concerning Nostalgic Influences on Consumer Tastes," *Journal of Business Research* 37 (September 1996)1: 27–40.

20 Stacy Menzel Baker, Holli C. Karrer, and Ann Veeck, "My Favorite Recipes: Recreating Emotions and Memories Through Cooking," *Advances in Consumer Research* vol. 32, no. 1 (2005): 304–305.

Truth 9

21 Mary Kay Ericksen and M. Joseph Sirgy, "Achievement Motivation and Clothing Preferences of White-Collar Working Women," in Michael R. Solomon, ed., *The Psychology of Fashion* (Lexington, MA: Lexington Books, 1985), 357–369.

22 "Survey Tells Why Gardening's Good," *Vancouver Sun* (April 12, 1997): B12.

Truth 10

23 Russell W. Belk, "Possessions and the Extended Self," *Journal of Consumer Research* 15 (September 1988): 139–168; Melanie Wallendorf and Eric J. Arnould, "'My Favorite Things': A Cross-Cultural Inquiry into Object Attachment, Possessiveness, and Social Linkage," *Journal of Consumer Research* 14 (March 1988): 531–547; http://observer.guardian.co.uk/uk_news/story/0,6903,1562293,00.html, accessed June 30, 2007; cf. also www.organicfood.co.uk/inspiration/downshifting and www.handbag.com/careers/careerchange/downshifting/ June 30, 2007.

24 Marsha L. Richins, "Special Possessions and the Expression of Material Values," *Journal of Consumer Research* 21 (December 1994): 522–533.

25 David Brooks, "Why BoBos Rule," *Newsweek* (April 3, 2000): 62–64.

Truth 11

26 Emily Burg, "Whole Foods Is Consumers' Favorite Green Brand," *Marketing Daily*, mediapost.com, accessed May 10, 2007.

27 www.lohas.com/about.html, accessed June 30, 2007.

28 Adrienne W. Fawcett, "Conscientious Consumerism Drives Record New Product Launches in 2006," nytimes.com/magazine, accessed January 24, 2007.

29 Sarah Mahoney, "Wal-Mart: The Average Joe Is Greener Than You Think," *Marketing Daily*, available from mediapost.com, accessed April 19, 2007.

30 http://green.yahoo.com/index.php?q=action, accessed June 30, 2007.

Truth 12

31 Gary Rivlin, "Facing the World with Egos Exposed," *New York Times Online* (June 3, 2004).

32 Marsha L. Richins, "Social Comparison and the Idealized Images of Advertising," *Journal of Consumer Research* 18 (June 1991): 71–83; Mary C. Martin and Patricia F. Kennedy, "Advertising and Social Comparison: Consequences for Female Preadolescents and Adolescents," *Psychology & Marketing* 10 (November–December 1993): 513–530.

33 Philip N. Myers, Jr. and Frank A. Biocca, "The Elastic Body Image: The Effect of Television Advertising and Programming on Body Image Distortions in Young Women," *Journal of Communication* 42 (Summer 1992): 108–133.

34 Charles S. Gulas and Kim McKeage, "Extending Social Comparison: An Examination of the Unintended Consequences of Idealized Advertising Imagery," *Journal of Advertising* 29 (Summer 2000): 17–28.

Truth 14

35 A. L. E. Birdwell, "A Study of Influence of Image Congruence on Consumer Choice," *Journal of Business* 41 (January 1964): 76–88; Edward L. Grubb and Gregg Hupp, "Perception of Self, Generalized Stereotypes, and Brand Selection," *Journal of Marketing Research* 5 (February 1986): 58–63.

36 Benedict Carey, "With That Saucy Swagger, She Must Drive a Porsche," *New York Times Online* (June 13, 2006).

37 Russell W. Belk, "Shoes and Self," *Advances in Consumer Research* (2003): 27–33.

Truth 15

38 Diane Goldner, "What Men and Women Really Want...to Eat," *New York Times* (March 2, 1994): C1 (2).

39 "Defining Metro Sexuality" *Metrosource* (September/October/November 2003).

40 "National Poll Reveals the Emergence of a 'New Man,'" Millerbrewing.com, accessed April 15, 2006.

Truth 20

41 Linda Keslar, "What's in a Name?" *Individual Investor* (April 1999): 101–102.

42 Seth Stevenson, "How to Beat Nike," *New York Times Online* (January 5, 2003).

43 Gabriel Kahn, "Philips Blitzes Asian Market as It Strives to Become Hip," *Wall Street Journal Online* (August 1, 2002).

44 Erin White, "Volvo Sheds Safe Image for New, Dangerous Ads," *Wall Street Journal Online* (June 14, 2002).

Truth 21

45 "Consumers Willing to Trade Off Privacy for Electronic Personalization," www.mediapost.com, accessed January 23, 2007.

Truth 23

46 Julie Bosman, "Chevy Tries a Write-Your-Own-Ad Approach, and the Potshots Fly," *The New York Times* (April 4, 2006).

Truth 25

47 Gary Belsky, "Why Smart People Make Major Money Mistakes," *Money* (July 1995): 76; Richard Thaler and Eric J. Johnson, "Gambling with the House Money or Trying to Break Even: The Effects of Prior Outcomes on Risky Choice," *Management Science* 36 (June 1990): 643–660; Richard Thaler, "Mental Accounting and Consumer Choice," *Marketing Science* 4 (Summer 1985): 199–214.

48 Geoffrey C. Kiel and Roger A. Layton, "Dimensions of Consumer Information Seeking Behavior," *Journal of Marketing Research* 28 (May 1981): 233–239.

49 Richard Thaler, "Mental Accounting and Consumer Choice," *Marketing Science* 4 (Summer 1985): 199–214, quoted on p. 206.

Truth 27

50 "Customer Product Reviews Drive Online Satisfaction and Conversion," www.mediapost.com (January 24, 2007).

Truth 28

51 John et al., "Sampling Data for Covariation Assessment: The Effects of Prior Beliefs on Search Patterns," *Journal of Consumer Research* 13 (June 1986): 1;38–48.

Truth 29

52 John P. Robinson, "Time Squeeze," *Advertising Age* (February 1990): 30–33.

53 "We're Hating the Waiting; 43% Prefer Self-Service," *Marketing Daily* (January 23, 2007), mediapost.com.

Truth 30

54 Gary L. Clark, Peter F. Kaminski, and David R. Rink, "Consumer Complaints: Advice on How Companies Should Respond Based on an Empirical Study," *Journal of Services Marketing* 6 (Winter 1992): 41–50.

Truth 31

55 Dyan Machan, "Is the Hog Going Soft?" *Forbes* (March 10, 1997): 114–119.

Truth 36

56 Lawrence F. Feick, Linda L. Price, and Robin A. Higie, "People Who Use People: The Other Side of Opinion Leadership," in Richard J. Lutz, ed., *Advances in Consumer Research* 13 (Provo, UT: Association for Consumer Research, 1986): 301–305.

57 Scale items adapted from Lawrence F. Feick and Linda L. Price, "The Market Maven: A Diffuser of Marketplace Information," *Journal of Marketing* 51 (January 1987): 83–87.

Truth 37

58 Barbara Kiviat, "The End of Management," *Time Inside Business* (July 12, 2004). [http://www.time.com/time/magazine/article/0,9171,994658,00.html] , accessed October 5, 2007.

Truth 38

59 Robert Lohrer, "Haggar Targets Women with $8M Media Campaign," *Daily News Record* (January 8, 1997): 1.

60 Jennifer Steinhauer, "Mars and Venus: Who Is 'the Decider'?" *New York Times Online* (April 26, 2006), accessed April 26, 2006; "Tailor-Made," *Advertising Age* (September 23, 2002): 14.

Truth 39

61 "Kids Strongly Influence Brand Decisions," www.marketingpower. com (February 22, 2007).

62 Russell N. Laczniak and Kay M. Palan, "Under the Influence," *Marketing Research* (Spring 2004): 34–39.

63 Stephanie Thompson, "Mrs. Butterworth's Changes Her Target," *Advertising Age* (December 20, 1999): 44.

Truth 40

64 Steve Kroft, "The Echo Boomers," CBSNews.com (October 3, 2004), accessed October 3, 2004.

65 Laurel Anderson and Julie L. Ozanne, "The Cyborg Teen: Identity Play and Deception on the Internet," *Advances in Consumer Research* 33, no. 1 (2006).

Truth 41

66 Amy Merrick, "Gap Plans Five Forth & Towne Stores for Fall," *The Wall Street Journal* (April 22, 2005): B1.

Truth 43

67 Shelly Reese, "The Many Faces of Affluence," *Marketing Tools* (November–December 1997): 44–48.

68 Martin Fackler, "Pajamas: Not Just for Sleep Anymore," *Opelika-Auburn News* (September 13, 2002): 7A.

Truth 45

69 Robert V. Kozinets, "Utopian Enterprise: Articulating the Meanings of *Star Trek*'s Culture of Consumption," *Journal of Consumer Research* 28 (June 2001): 67–88, quoted on p.74.

About the Author

Michael R. Solomon, Ph.D. is Professor of Marketing and Director of the Center for Consumer Research in the Haub School of Business at Saint Joseph's University in Philadelphia. He is also Professor of Consumer Behaviour at the Manchester School of Business, The University of Manchester, U.K. Professor Solomon's primary research interests include consumer behavior and lifestyle issues, branding strategy, symbolic aspects of products, psychology of fashion, decoration, and image, services marketing, and the development of visually oriented online research methodologies. Professor Solomon has been recognized as one of the 15 most widely cited scholars in the academic behavioral sciences and fashion literature and as one of the 10 most productive scholars in the field of advertising and marketing communications. His textbook, *Consumer Behavior: Buying, Having, and Being*, published by Prentice Hall, is widely used in universities throughout North America, Europe, and Australia and is now in its eighth edition.

In addition to his academic activities, Professor Solomon is a frequent contributor to mass media. His feature articles have appeared in magazines such as *Psychology Today*, *Gentleman's Quarterly*, and *Savvy*. He has been quoted in numerous national magazines and newspapers, including *Allure*, *Elle*, *Glamour*, *Mademoiselle*, *Mirabella*, *Newsweek*, *The New York Times*, *Self*, *USA Today*, and *The Wall Street Journal*. He frequently appears on television and radio to comment on consumer behavior issues, including *The Today Show*, *Good Morning America*, CNBC, Channel One, *Inside Edition*, *Newsweek on the Air*, *The Wall Street Journal* Radio Network, the *Entrepreneur Sales and Marketing* show, the WOR Radio Network, and National Public Radio. Professor Solomon provides input as a marketing consultant to a variety of organizations on issues related to consumer behavior, branding, services marketing, retailing, and advertising. He frequently speaks to business organizations around the world about new trends in consumer behavior.

Simply the best thinking

THE TRUTH AND NOTHING BUT THE TRUTH

The **Truth About** Series offers the collected and distilled knowledge on a topic and shows you how you to apply this knowledge in your everyday life.

Learn real solutions for problems faced by every manager in this definitive, evidence-based guide to effective management.

ISBN: 0132346036
Stephen P. Robbins
$18.99

Dynamic, effective public speaking is the gateway to professional and personal success. It's not easy, but it's a skill you can develop.

ISBN: 0132354969
James O'Rourke
$18.99

This book distills the entire field of brand management into what you need to succeed!

ISBN: 0137128169
Brian D. Till and Donna Heckler
$18.99

Also Available

The Truth About Avoiding Scams
The Truth About Hiring the Best
The Truth About Negotiations
The Truth About Thriving in Change